# Storytelling in the SEO Age

## A Nonfiction Writer's Guide to Success.

II

# Storytelling In The SEO Age

*A Nonfiction Writer's Guide to Success.*

James R Martin

Real Deal Press

J R Martin Media Inc/Real Deal Press

JR@jrmartinmedia.com

Publisher's Cataloging-in-Publication

Martin, James R.

Storytelling in the SEO Age  A Nonfiction Writer's Guide to Success / by James R. Martin -- 1st edition.

cm.

Includes bibliographic references and index.

LCCN

ISBN-13: 979-8-9875933-87


1. Nonfiction Writing --Author

2. English - Production and direction

3. Multimedia (Art)--Production and direction

4. .Storytelling    .I. Title.

## Trademarks

All terms mentioned in this book that are known to be trademarks or service marks have been appropriately capitalized. The author and the publisher can not attest to the accuracy of this information. Use of a term in this book should not be regarded as affecting the validity of any trademark or service mark.

## Photographs and Illustrations

Unless otherwise noted and credited all photographs and illustrations are original copyrighted works of the author or public domain.

## Fair Use Notice

This book may contain material the use of which has not always been specifically authorized by the copyright owner. Such material is being used in an effort to educationally advance understanding of environmental, political, human rights, economic, democratic, scientific, social justice, authoring, writing and documentary issues etc. We believe this constitutes a "fair use" of any such copyrighted materials as provided for in section 107 of the US copyright law.

## Warning and Disclaimer

Every effort has been made to make this book as complete and as accurate as possible, but no warranty or fitness is implied. The author and the publisher shall have neither liability, nor responsibility to any person or entity with respect to any loss or damage arising from the information contained in this book.

## About The Author

James R. Martin is a distinguished author and Emmy-award-winning writer, director, and producer recognized for his compelling film, television, and digital media contributions. With an expanding publishing career, Jim has authored several well-received books, including "Documentary Directing and Storytelling" and "Actuality Interviewing and Listening." As he ventures further into the literary world, his legacy in filmmaking continues to enhance his storytelling prowess. In his seventh book, he writes about what a nonfiction writer needs to know in many crucial areas. It's a guide to writing nonfiction based on what he has learned writing in many genres and disciplines.

Film credits include two Emmy nominations and an Emmy Award for nationally aired PBS documentary- Fired-up Public Housing is My Home."

## Other Books by James R. Martin

### Nonfiction

- Create Documentary Films, Videos and Multimedia 3rd Edition.
- Actuality Interviewing and Listening.
- Listen, Learn, Share.
- Office and Home Tai Chi with Yue Zhang. Translator, writer, and editor English Edition,
- The Shaolin Temple Story, Translator, writer and     editor, with Hongyun Sun. Author Shi Yongxin.

### Fiction

- Silhouettes and Shadows, "Humanity Follows the Earth, Earth Follows the Universe."

# Contents

## Contents Continued:

## Acknowledgements

I'm deeply grateful to my family, friends, and everyone who's been there for me with their unwavering support and encouragement. A special shoutout to my son Aaron, who never hesitates to give me the honest feedback I sometimes need.

To all my readers, your engagement with my books fills my heart with appreciation. Thank you for being part of my journey.

# FORWARD

Welcome to the captivating domain of nonfiction writing! In this comprehensive book, you will embark on a thrilling journey of exploration, creativity, and self-expression. Whether you're a seasoned professional writer, aspiring to become one, or seeking to enhance your communication skills, this guide is your gateway to crafting compelling nonfiction narratives that resonate with readers.

Throughout these pages, you will unlock the art of storytelling through real-life events, experiences, and captivating ideas. Nonfiction encompasses many genres and styles, each offering a unique perspective. Subjects range from fascinating memoirs and biographies to thought-provoking essays and compelling journalism. This book will act as your compass, providing invaluable tools, knowledge, and inspiration to unearth the stories within you and empower you to share them with the world.

During your enriching journey, you will master breathing life into your narratives, skillfully engaging readers with your authentic voice, and transforming ordinary moments into extraordinary tales. Dive into the research process, discover how to gather information, and incorporate keywords for search engine optimization (SEO). Conduct impeccable fact-checking, ensuring your nonfiction works are grounded in truth and accuracy.

However, this guide is more than just about the mechanics of writing. It's about discovering your distinct perspective and voice and leveraging it to forge deep connections with readers. Uncover the awe-inspiring power of storytelling to inspire, educate, and ignite change. Dive into the ethical responsibilities of nonfiction writing, understanding the significance of empathy, fairness, and respect for the individuals and communities you portray.

As you progress through the book, immerse yourself in invigorating self-generated writing exercises and those suggested in the book. Review your work based on insights from reading about the work of seasoned nonfiction writers who have indelibly left their mark on the literary realm. Share your work with family, friends, and editors for feedback. Be encouraged to experiment, take risks, and embrace the joy of discovery as you refine your craft.

A writer's journey is about reaching a destination and reveling in the process. So, grasp your pen, open your mind, and get ready to embark on a transformative adventure. Explore the vast landscapes of nonfiction writing, unearth hidden stories, and share your unique perspective. Let the journey of a lifetime begin!

## PREFACE

Writing is a pursuit that requires more than wanting to do it. It requires a command of language, style, and the ability to communicate your thoughts. It isn't easy, even if you have talent, education, and a vocabulary. In the art world, primitive artists create works of art. But I am not aware of any primitive writers. Despite your experience, education, or talent, you must, as they say, "put pen to paper" and see what happens. At the same time, you must also find your voice. Educate yourself in the craft of writing. By doing so, you may discover the writer you want to be.

Writing is a learning process for the author and the reader. This book is based on a lifetime of writing for different purposes, most recently writing nonfiction books. I have also written screenplays, and a novel, course outlines, articles, and other assignments. Each writing assignment has unique requirements that require more learning. Writing a social media post requires priorities different from writing a letter to a friend.

I've always had a passion for writing in various forms. Whether it's crafting screenplays for my films, outlining courses, or authoring books, writing and reading have been at the core of my creative pursuits. When making documentaries, we often strive to present the objective truth, showcasing the facts and capturing reality as it is, which I like to call "actuality." However, the truth is that it's nearly impossible to achieve pure objectivity because we, as human beings, are inherently subjective.

The best approach to our nonfiction writing may be acknowledging our subjectivity and actively recognizing its influence on our perspectives. By doing so, we become more aware of our biases and can explore how they shape our understanding of reality. This self-awareness empowers us to navigate our subjectivity and strive for a more nuanced portrayal of the world that reflects our unique perspective while also seeking a connection to a broader, universal reality.

Ultimately, it's about finding that delicate balance between our subjectivity and the pursuit of truth. By embracing and consciously examining our subjectivity, we can engage with our audiences more honestly and authentically, offering them a glimpse into a reality that holds personal significance and resonates on a deeper, shared level.

Today there is much talk about Artificial Intelligence (AI) and its influence on writing. AI does not possess personal experiences or beliefs but can offer insights into the subject matter. When I queried Chat GPT Open AI, it responded with the following ideas.

*"Human beings, like AI, are indeed influenced by various factors from birth that shape their perspectives and biases. When it comes to artificial intelligence, it's important to recognize that the subjectivity lies not within the AI itself but in the humans who design and program it. The biases and subjective viewpoints of the creators can inadvertently be embedded into the AI's algorithms and data inputs."*

*"However, there are ways in which artificial intelligence can strive to overcome subjectivity. One approach is through a diverse and inclusive design process. By involving*

individuals with a wide range of backgrounds, perspectives, and experiences, it's possible to mitigate the influence of specific biases and foster a more balanced and objective AI system. Additionally, ongoing AI algorithm monitoring, testing, and refining can help identify and rectify emerging biases."

"While AI can aim for objectivity in its decision-making processes, it ultimately operates within the parameters and data it has been given. Therefore, even with the best efforts to minimize bias, AI systems are not immune to inheriting subjective tendencies from their human creators. The key lies in continuous improvement, transparency, and responsible development practices to ensure that AI technology evolves toward greater fairness, inclusivity, and objectivity (Chat GPT -Open AI 2023)."

Understanding the programming used for AI can guide the use of it for nonfiction writing. It reminds us that nonfiction is, by default, subjective. We can take this into account when we write. AI is a resource for research, analysis, and perspective. It can be an aid in refining your thoughts and writing.

This book is meant to explore many aspects of nonfiction writing. But the techniques apply to any form of storytelling. A short paragraph on a social media site like "Tribel" must tell a story as much as a nonfiction book does. Translating reality, experiences, and history into words requires talent, skill, and language understanding.

As the author of this book, I aim to share my knowledge and what I've learned thus far to help you achieve your writing ambitions. Read this book and use the information to help you write your book or other project. It is a guide and short course on nonfiction writing. It will help you gain insight into nonfiction writing that you can use now.

Happy reading, learning, and writing!

# CHAPTER 1

## Introduction to Nonfiction Storytelling Style, Tone and Search Engine Optimization (SEO)

**Please read each of the following three paragraphs.**

### Version One

Step into the realm of boundless creativity, where the power of your words can shape the world around you. Within the pages of this transformative guide, I extend my hand to guide you on a remarkable journey—an expedition into the captivating realm of nonfiction storytelling. Together, we will unravel the secrets of crafting a compelling narrative that breathes life into the concepts and ideas swirling within your mind. Listen closely, for within these words lies the key to unlocking the potential that resides within you. Discover the vital starting point, the foundation upon which your story will unfold—through writing. Allow me to illuminate the path that leads from the ethereal realm of imagination to the tangible realm of the written word. Just as a scattered jigsaw puzzle yearns to be assembled, your story yearns to be captured and brought to life. But unlike any puzzle, the beauty of your creation lies not only in the completion but also in the choices you make along the way. Armed with the knowledge and wisdom you will gain about storytelling, you shall lay the first piece on the table, igniting a journey that will forever alter the trajectory of your writing endeavors. Are you ready to embrace the power within and embark on this extraordinary expedition?

### Key words and phrases used in version one.

- Boundless creativity
- Power of your words
- Transformative guide
- Remarkable journey
- Nonfiction storytelling
- Crafting a compelling narrative
- Concepts and ideas
- Unlocking potential
- Knowledge
- Ethereal realm of imagination
- Tangible realm of the written word
- Jigsaw puzzle
- Storytelling
- Writing endeavors
- Extraordinary expedition.
- Starting point

## Version Two

I'm here to help you write a nonfiction story conveying a concept or idea in your mind. What you learn will help you find a place to start --to commit words to paper or a computer screen. After all, is said and done, you must write your thoughts down. Otherwise, the story you envision only exists as a random musing in your mind. It can only be a story if you write it down and see where it goes. In one way, it is like the picture of a landscape on a puzzle box. It can only exist if you put the pieces together. But unlike the picture puzzle, your story can have whatever look and feel you create. Not only do you need to solve the puzzle to complete the picture, but you must also decide what the picture will be. Based on what you know and learn about storytelling, it begins when you put that first puzzle piece on the table.

## Version Three (Keywords Added)

"I'm here to guide you on your nonfiction writing journey, imparting essential knowledge and skills to articulate an idea or concept you wish to explore. As you delve into the art of nonfiction writing, you'll uncover the starting point from which you can transpose your thoughts onto paper or a digital platform. The act of writing breathes life into your ideas. Otherwise, the narratives you imagine remain elusive thoughts, fragments of potential stories. Nonfiction writing is akin to assembling a jigsaw puzzle using a landscape image as a guide. Yet, in your writing, the final image is not predetermined; it's a dynamic creation that evolves with every word you write, with every 'puzzle piece' you place in your narrative. With the acquired knowledge about nonfiction storytelling, your journey commences when you lay down the first puzzle piece—your initial sentence—in the vast landscape of your nonfiction narrative."

**SEO Keywords used in version three:** Nonfiction writing, *imparting knowledge, articulate idea, writing journey, starting point, digital platform, elusive thoughts, potential stories, narrative, acquired knowledge, nonfiction storytelling.*

## Comparison Version One, Two, and Three

Comparing the first two paragraphs, we find the first paragraph has a more grandiose, poetic writing style. It uses evocative language and imagery to create a sense of wonder and adventure. The inspirational tone encourages readers to embrace their creative potential and embark on a transformative journey. It has sixteen Search Engine

Optimization (SEO) keywords included. The point of considering SEO for your book is that readers looking for the subject of your writing can find it online. It's essential in descriptions of the book or the forward to include keywords in your writing.

## Keywords

The keywords in version one reflect specific ideas and themes within the text and are likely to be terms people search for when seeking content on this subject.

These keywords reflect the key ideas and themes within the text and are likely to be terms people search for when seeking content on this subject. Certain retailers like Amazon rely on the keywords (or short phrases) used in your book's listing and description. Amazon's search algorithms factor in up to seven keywords or phrases when someone searches looking for books with subjects they are interested in.

The title and subtitle of the book are essential and include keywords. But the entire package of title, subtitle, description, and keywords represent the book everywhere. Consider the following steps to research keywords for your book.

- *Books that are like your book.*
- *Keywords or phrases people might use to find or search those books.*
- *Use Google, Amazon, or other venues to search with those keywords or phrases.*
- *See which titles appear in the top twenty selections.*

- Consider the top five keywords or phrases and use them prompted to enter keywords in various book setup programs.

- If necessary, repeat this process to refine your process. You may decide to change your title and subtitle to incorporate new keywords.

The **second version,** on the other hand, has a more straightforward and direct writing style. It presents the information, focusing on practical advice and the importance of acting. The tone is more instructional and emphasizes the necessity of writing down thoughts to bring them to life. It uses the metaphor of a puzzle to illustrate the writing process and highlights the importance of solving the problem and deciding on the outcome.

The *third version* adds more descriptive language to the second paragraph and includes more substantial search engine optimization (SEO) content.

Overall, the *first version* is more expressive and aimed at creating an emotional connection with the reader. If the reader views the writing as too flamboyant, it is possible they will not take it seriously. In contrast, the second paragraph is more informational and focused on providing guidance and practical insights. It runs the risk of not engaging the reader. However, it will help potential readers find the content.

Each version has a place in nonfiction story writing. The first paragraph style would be inappropriate for a factual newspaper article. It might be great for opening a nonfiction story and inviting readers to embark on an adventurous learning experience. The second paragraph is direct and appropriate but might benefit from some emotional context. The third paragraph offers a middle ground

**First Exercise: Please write your version of the previous paragraphs or something original, using your language and writing style.**

**Here's a pure third-person approach to the same introductory paragraphs:**

The purpose of this book is learning how to craft nonfiction stories. Creating storytelling that effectively communicates a concept or idea in the reader's mind. The knowledge acquired through this process will aid in identifying a starting point in your writing, whether transcribing thoughts onto paper or typing them onto a computer screen. This is a crucial step without which the envisioned story remains open to random notions within the mind. It needs the form and substance of an actual narrative. Just like a landscape image depicted on a puzzle box, the story can only manifest when its constituent parts are assembled. However, unlike the fixed picture puzzle, the writer can shape the story's appearance and atmosphere according to their preferences. Solving the problem entails making deliberate choices about its content. Drawing upon the insights gained from this study of storytelling, the journey commences with the placement of the initial puzzle piece on the table, setting the foundation for the narrative to unfold.

## Storytelling

Let's dive right into the world of storytelling! Whether you're writing fiction or nonfiction, key elements apply to all types of stories. While fiction writing takes us into the realms of imagination, nonfiction stays grounded, relying on facts and avoiding unsubstantiated opinions and falsehoods. The way you tell your story draws upon timeless storytelling traditions. Let's say you're crafting a nonfiction book about unraveling a scientific mystery. Are you primarily focused on revealing the answer to the puzzle or showcasing the intriguing process of solving it? It could be both. Now, one of the first things you'll want to do is find a captivating "hook" to grab your readers' attention and keep them engrossed. We'll delve into hooks, concepts, and treatments as we go along, but first, let's set the stage with some "backstory."

When it comes to telling a nonfiction story, the possibilities are endless! You can write a book or bring it to life visually through a film, video, exhibit, or even a captivating series of photographs. If you feel artistic, you can use drawings, animations, or paintings to convey your narrative in book form. You can also get creative with presentations using slides or immerse your audience in an exhibit. How far can you go with this idea? Today there are many television shows classified as "nonfiction using actors and recreated scenes. Theatrical nonfiction is technically fiction but based on actual people, events, and facts. The musical "Hamilton" is a prime example of this concept. While it takes creative liberties and artistic interpretations, it is grounded in historical events and characters.

"Hamilton" tells the story of Alexander Hamilton, one of America's founding fathers, and his role in shaping the nation's early history. The musical incorporates various historical figures, such as George Washington, Thomas Jefferson, and Aaron Burr, who interact with Hamilton throughout the narrative. It draws heavily from Ron Chernow's biography of Hamilton, which serves as a primary source of historical information.

In prioritizing actual people, events, and facts, "Hamilton" demonstrates a significant commitment to historical accuracy. Lin-Manuel Miranda, the creator and composer of the musical conducted extensive research on Hamilton's life and the events of the time. This research forms the foundation upon which the narrative and characters are built.

It is important to note that "Hamilton" also employs elements of artistic license and fictional storytelling techniques. Miranda intentionally takes creative liberties with historical events, character portrayals, and the overall structure of the musical. This artistic interpretation allows the show to transcend a mere historical reenactment and become a vibrant and engaging theater piece.

For example, casting actors from diverse backgrounds, with many of them portraying historically white characters, adds a contemporary and inclusive layer to the story. Additionally, the music in "Hamilton" incorporates a blend of hip-hop, R&B, and other modern musical styles, which deviates from the traditional sounds associated with the period. This fusion of musical genres not only makes the show more accessible to a modern audience but also enhances its emotional impact.

While "Hamilton" may deviate from strict historical accuracy at times, its principal goal, besides entertainment, is to educate and inspire audiences about a crucial period in American history. By intertwining fiction and reality, the musical brings historical figures and events to life in a way that resonates with contemporary audiences, making the story relatable and relevant. The musical "Hamilton" exemplifies the concept of theatrical nonfiction by blending fictional elements with historical facts. While it takes artistic liberties, it remains grounded in the lives of real people and the events that shaped the birth of the United States. Through its creative storytelling and artistic choices, "Hamilton" prioritizes historical authenticity while captivating and engaging audiences.

Individuals demonstrate the power of words spoken aloud to an audience in a talk or lecture! Nonfiction stories often revolve around real people who play different roles—individuals, groups, or entire communities. These characters take center stage, propelling the story forward with their actions and choices. To make the story feel authentic, it's usually set in real-world locations like bustling cities, vast countries, or breathtaking natural environments. The setting provides a backdrop and influences the characters' behavior and motivations.

Nonfiction stories explore a wide range of subjects, from the wonders of nature to the intricacies of science and beyond. They are all connected to how we, as humans, live and perceive the universe around us. Sometimes, the subject or topic of the nonfiction story becomes the main character, captivating our attention and guiding us through their journey. An excellent nonfiction story thrives on a clear and compelling story line rooted in actual events and experiences. The plot should be well-structured, taking us on an exciting journey that includes a beginning, middle, and end that  provides a satisfying resolution. Nonfiction stories often delve into significant themes and address critical issues, such as social justice, human rights, or environmentalism. The theme serves as the underlying message or moral of the story, leaving a lasting impact on the reader or viewer.

Typically, nonfiction stories are told from a specific perspective, such as the author's, a character's, or a topic's perspective. The point of view can influence the reader's interpretation of the story and create a sense of intimacy or distance. The author should make the point of view of the story clear. Consider which writing style is best for your story. It may be that a combination of techniques can be used. In the following section, we review writing styles.

## Critical Elements of a Conversational Writing Style

### Informal Tone

Use a casual and relaxed tone, as if speaking directly to the reader. Avoid overly formal language and opt for a friendly and approachable voice.

### Use of Contractions

Incorporate contractions (e.g., "don't," "can't," "won't") to mimic natural speech patterns and make the writing sound more conversational.

### Shorter Sentences

Break up complex ideas into more concise, easily digestible sentences. This helps maintain a conversational flow and prevents the writing from becoming too dense or overwhelming. Avoid run-on sentences.

### Personal Pronouns

Address the reader directly using pronouns like "you" and "we" to create a sense of connection and engagement. It makes the reader feel like an active participant in the conversation.

## Conversational Phrases

Incorporate common idiomatic phrases and expressions, such as "let's," "I mean," "you know," and "by the way," to add a natural, informal touch to the writing. However, this can quickly become tedious and cliché. It is more appropriate for dialog between individuals in a fictional context.

## Rhetorical Questions

Pose rhetorical questions to engage the reader and encourage them to think or reflect on a particular topic. It adds an interactive element to the writing and simulates a conversational dialogue.

## Use of Examples and Stories

Share relatable examples and anecdotes to illustrate your points and make the content more relatable. Storytelling helps create a conversational narrative and keeps the reader engaged.

## Active Voice

Utilize the active voice to make the writing more dynamic and direct. It adds clarity and emphasizes the subject's action, making the writing more conversational and engaging.

## Emotion and Humor

Infuse the writing with emotion and occasional humor to create a connection with the reader. This helps to establish rapport and maintain interest throughout the conversation.

## Authenticity

Be yourself and write in a way that feels natural to you. Authenticity in your voice and tone enhances the conversational style and builds trust with the reader.

Remember, conversational writing aims to emulate a friendly and engaging conversation between the writer and the reader. It should be accessible, relatable, and easy to follow, inviting the reader to participate in the discussion actively.

## Critical Elements of a First-person Writing Style

### Pronouns

Use first-person pronouns like "I," "me," "my," and "we" to directly address the reader and establish a personal connection. This perspective allows writers to share their experiences, thoughts, and emotions.

### Personal Voice

Emphasize the writer's unique voice and perspective throughout the piece. This helps create an intimate and subjective narrative that reflects the writer's individuality and personal understanding of the subject matter.

### Subjectivity

Presenting the story or information from the writer's point of view, highlighting their personal opinions, beliefs, and biases, and acknowledging that this perspective may not be universally applicable or objective is essential.

### Reflective Tone

Adopt a thoughtful and introspective tone to explore the writer's thoughts, feelings, and experiences. This introspection can provide deeper insights into the subject matter and create a more engaging and relatable narrative.

### Use of Personal Anecdotes

Incorporate personal anecdotes and experiences to illustrate points, provide examples, or support arguments.

These stories add authenticity and allow the reader to connect with the writer personally.

## Emotional Expression

Express emotions openly and honestly, sharing the writer's reactions, joys, sorrows, and challenges. By conveying personal feelings, the writing becomes more engaging and resonates with the reader's emotional experiences.

## Informal Language

Adopt a conversational and informal language style similar to speaking in everyday conversations. Only overly formal or technical language if it aligns with the writer's natural voice and the purpose of the piece.

## Intimate Perspective

Provide a sense of closeness and familiarity by sharing personal details or insights that deepen the reader's understanding of the writer's thoughts and experiences. This perspective can help create a strong bond between the writer and the reader.

## Limited Knowledge

Acknowledge that the writer's knowledge and understanding are limited to their experiences and perspective. Avoid presenting opinions or personal experiences as universal truths, recognizing the inherent subjectivity of the first-person narrative.

## Authenticity

Be true to yourself and maintain authenticity throughout the writing. By embracing vulnerability and sharing genuine thoughts and experiences, the first-person writing style can create a powerful and relatable connection with the reader.

The first-person writing style allows the writer to share their experiences, thoughts, and emotions directly with the reader. It is an intimate and subjective approach that invites the reader into the writer's world and perspective, fostering a sense of trust and authenticity.

## Critical Elements of a Third-person Writing style.

### Pronouns

Use third-person pronouns like "he," "she," "it," "they," or the character's name to refer to individuals or entities within the narrative. This creates a sense of objectivity and distance from the writer.

### Objective Perspective

Maintain an objective and impartial viewpoint throughout the writing. The narrator or writer observes and reports on the characters' actions, thoughts, and emotions without directly inserting their opinions or experiences.

### External Observations

Present the story or information from an external perspective, describing events and characters from an observer's point of view. The focus is on depicting the external actions and behaviors rather than delving into the character's internal thoughts and emotions.

### Consistent Tone

Maintain a consistent tone throughout the piece, matching the overall mood and atmosphere of the narrative. The style can be formal, informal, serious, or light-hearted, depending on the context and genre.

## Omniscient or Limited Perspective

Choose between an omniscient point of view, where the narrator has complete knowledge of all characters' thoughts and feelings, or a limited perspective, where the narrator only has access to the thoughts and feelings of one or a few characters.

## Descriptive Language

Use descriptive language to create vivid imagery and provide details about the characters, settings, and events. This helps the reader visualize the story and immerse themselves in the narrative.

## Character Development

Develop characters through their actions, dialogue, and interactions with others. Show their personality traits, motivations, and relationships through external cues rather than explicitly stating their thoughts and emotions.

## Authorial Voice

Maintain a consistent authorial voice that reflects the overall style and tone of the narrative. Your voice should be distinct and engaging, drawing the reader into the story while remaining separate from the characters.

## Balanced Perspective

Present a balanced view of the characters and events, avoiding bias or favoritism. Provide enough information for the reader to form their own opinions and interpretations.

## Clarity and Coherence

Ensure the narrative is clear and coherent, allowing the reader to follow the story and understand the events and relationships between characters. Smooth transitions between scenes and logical progression of events are essential.

The third-person writing style creates a sense of objectivity and detachment from the writer, allowing for an external perspective on the story. It effectively conveys the narrative by focusing on external observations, character actions, and descriptive language. The third-person style provides a balanced and engaging storytelling experience for the reader by maintaining consistency and clarity.

### Example: Conversational Third-person Writing Style

"Imagine you're strolling down the bustling streets of a vibrant city. People rush by, their footsteps echoing on the pavement as fresh coffee wafts through the air. The city comes alive with a symphony of sounds, from car horns blaring to the laughter of children playing in the nearby park. It's a scene that captures the energy and diversity of urban life."

"As you observe the vibrant cityscape, you notice a group of street performers gathering on a corner. Their music fills the air, inviting passersby to pause and listen. A guitarist strums a catchy melody while a violinist adds a touch of elegance to the composition. The rhythm of drums reverberates through your body, urging you to tap your feet to the beat."

"Amidst the crowd, a young woman steps forward and starts to dance. Her movements are graceful and fluid, captivating everyone who watches. She embodies the music, her body swaying and twirling in perfect harmony.

The onlookers are mesmerized by her talent, their eyes fixed on her every move."

"In this vibrant city, filled with its eclectic mix of people and cultures, you realize that art has the power to transcend boundaries. It unites strangers, evokes emotions, and creates moments of shared beauty. As you continue your journey through the streets, you carry the memory of that captivating dance, a reminder of the magic that can be found in the most unexpected places."

In this example, the writing style adopts a conversational tone while maintaining a third-person perspective. The reader is engaged through descriptive language, inviting them to imagine themselves in the scene and experience the city's sights, sounds, and emotions. Using vivid imagery and relatable experiences helps connect the reader and the narrative, making it feel like a friendly conversation.

### Third-party, Informal Writing Style

Picture yourself strolling down the lively streets of a bustling city. The whole place is buzzing with activity—people hurrying by their footsteps echoing on the pavement and the aroma of freshly brewed coffee floating through the air. It's like a symphony of sounds, with car horns blaring and children's laughter echoing from the nearby park. This scene captures the vibrant energy and diverse essence of urban life.

As you take in the lively cityscape, you can't help but notice a group of street performers gathering on a street corner. Their music fills the air, drawing in passersby, inviting them to pause and listen. A guitarist is strumming a catchy tune, and a violinist adds a touch of elegance to the mix. The beat of the drums resonates through your body, tempting you to tap your feet along.

Right amid the crowd, a young woman steps forward and starts dancing. Her movements are so graceful and fluid that she captivates everyone around her. She becomes one with the music, swaying and twirling in perfect harmony. The onlookers are spellbound by her talent. Their eyes are fixated on every captivating move she makes.

In this vibrant city, where people from all walks of life and cultures come together, you realize the true power of art. It can break boundaries, bring strangers together, evoke deep emotions, and create moments of shared beauty.

As you continue your journey through the city streets, you carry the memory of that enchanting dance with you, a reminder that true magic can be found in the most unexpected places.

### Example of Traditional Third-party Writing Style.

"As individuals stroll down the lively streets of the bustling city, the entire atmosphere is filled with vigorous activity. Footsteps echo on the pavement as people hurry past while the tantalizing scent of freshly brewed coffee permeates the air. The symphony of urban life resonates through the cacophony of sounds—car horns blaring and children's laughter reverberating from the nearby park. This bustling scene encapsulates the energy and diverse essence of the metropolis."

"The bustling cityscape offers a captivating sight to those who observe. Amidst the vibrant surroundings, a group of street performers has gathered on a street corner, their music permeating the atmosphere and enticing passersby to pause and notice. A skilled guitarist strums a catchy melody, complemented by the elegant strains of a violinist. The rhythmic beats of the drums compel onlookers to tap their feet in sync with the rhythm."

"In the heart of the crowd, a young woman steps forward, embarking on a captivating dance. Her movements are graceful and fluid, captivating the attention of all who look at her. She effortlessly embodies the music, her body swaying and twirling in perfect harmony. The mesmerized onlookers cannot tear their gaze away, their eyes fixed on every mesmerizing motion."

"Within this vibrant city, where individuals from diverse backgrounds and cultures converge, the profound power of art becomes evident. It transcends boundaries, bringing strangers together, evoking deep emotions, and creating moments of shared beauty. As individuals continue their journey through the bustling streets, they carry the memory of that enchanting dance, forever reminded of the wondrous magic that can be discovered in the unlikeliest of places."

### Critical Elements of a Second-person Writing Style.

### Pronouns:

Utilize second-person pronouns like "you" and "your" to directly address the reader as the narrative's protagonist. This creates a sense of personal involvement and engagement.

### Direct Address

Speak directly to the reader, involving them in the story or discussion. The writing should make the reader feel like an active participant or the narrative's main character.

## Instruction or Guidance

Provide instructions, advice, or guidance to the reader within the context of the narrative. The writing may offer suggestions, steps to follow, or recommendations tailored to the reader's actions or decisions.

## Inclusive Language

Use inclusive language to make the reader feel included and part of the experience. This can be achieved using words like "we" or "us" to create a sense of shared understanding or community.

## Immediacy

Create a sense of immediacy by using present tense or vivid descriptions that make the reader feel as if the events or actions are happening in the present moment. This helps to immerse the reader in the narrative.

## Empathy and Connection

Cultivate compassion and connect with readers by acknowledging their experiences, emotions, and motivations. The writing should resonate with the reader's perspective and make them feel understood.

## Rhetorical Questions

Pose rhetorical questions directly to the reader, encouraging them to reflect on their experiences, thoughts, or actions. This interactive element involves the reader in the writing process and promotes self-reflection.

## Encouragement and Motivation

Provide encouragement and motivation to the reader throughout the writing. This can involve inspiring the reader to act, overcome challenges, or embrace new perspectives.

## Clear and Concise Language

Use clear and concise language to communicate ideas effectively. The writing should be easy to understand and follow, ensuring that the reader remains engaged without confusion.

## Personalization

Tailor the writing to the reader's interests, needs, or desires. By addressing the reader directly, the writer can acknowledge their unique circumstances and offer personalized insights or recommendations.

Remember, the second-person writing style directly involves the reader by addressing them as the protagonist. It guides and instructs the reader, fostering a sense of personal connection and engagement. By using inclusive language, empathy, and personalized elements, the writing invites readers to actively participate in the narrative and apply the content to their experiences.

## The Use of Active and Passive Voices

The notion of "voice" is about whether the subject of a sentence or clause performs or receives the action. Understanding the differences in writing in an active or passive voice is essential. An active voice can be used to write about past or present things. However, it is most often considered writing in the present. When writing with an active voice, the sentence's subject acts, while in a passive voice, the subject receives the action.

**For example:**

Active voice: John threw the ball.
Passive voice: The ball was thrown by John.

In the active voice, "John" is the subject acting, while in the passive voice, the ball becomes the object receiving the action.

So why choose one over the other? Active voice is often preferred, making the writing more direct, clear, and engaging. It typically results in shorter, more concise sentences, conveying a sense of urgency and efficiency that keeps readers engaged.

Then again, there may also be instances where the passive voice is more appropriate, for example, when the focus needs to be on the object receiving the action more than who is performing the action or when the doer is not essential.

## Examples Active and Passive Voices

Passive voice: The glass was broken by a stray ball.

Active voice: A stray ball broke the glass.

In the previous example, the active voice emphasizes the ball as the subject, whereas the passive voice focuses on the glass. Therefore, using the active or passive voice is necessary based on what you want to emphasize in a sentence.

## Active Third-Person Voice

The researchers conducted experiments to test the new drug's effectiveness in treating the disease. They carefully analyzed the data collected from the participants and observed significant improvements in their symptoms. The findings indicate that the drug shows promising potential for relieving patients suffering from the disease.

## Passive Third-Person Voice

Experiments were conducted by the team of researchers to test the effectiveness of the new drug in treating the disease. The data collected from the participants were carefully analyzed, and significant improvements in their symptoms were observed. It is indicated by the findings that the drug shows promising potential for providing relief to patients suffering from the disease.

## Active First-Person Voice

I conducted experiments to test the new drug's effectiveness in treating the disease. I carefully analyzed the data collected from the participants and observed significant improvements in their symptoms. The findings indicate that the drug shows promising potential for relieving patients suffering from the disease.

## Passive First-Person Voice

Experiments were conducted by me to test the effectiveness of the new drug in treating the disease. The data collected from the participants were carefully analyzed by me, and significant improvements in their symptoms were observed. It is indicated by the findings that the drug shows promising potential for providing relief to patients suffering from the disease.

## Expository Narrative

Expository, narrative, and descriptive writing styles are distinct approaches, each with its purpose and characteristics. Here are the main differences between these writing styles.

## Purpose

The primary purpose of expository writing is to inform, explain, or instruct the reader about a specific topic or subject. It aims to provide facts, evidence, and logical explanations.

Narrative writing aims to tell a story or recount a series of events. Its purpose is to entertain, engage, or evoke emotions in the reader.

Descriptive writing seeks to create a vivid sensory experience by providing detailed descriptions of people, places, objects, or events. Its purpose is to paint a vivid picture in the reader's mind and evoke sensory and emotional responses.

## Structure

Expository writing follows a structured format, such as an introduction, body paragraphs, and a conclusion. It may include headings, subheadings, and a logical progression of ideas.

Narrative writing usually follows a chronological structure with a clear beginning, middle, and end. It may use a thematic form alone or incorporated in the chronological  It includes plot, characters, conflict, and resolution. Narrative writing may follow a nonlinear time format flashing back or forward in time to tell the story.

Descriptive writing does not follow a specific structure but focuses on sensory details and imagery. It uses figurative language, similes, metaphors, and other literary devices to create a vivid impression.

## Tone and Language

Expository writing tends to be objective, informative, and straightforward. It uses formal language, avoids personal opinions or biases, and relies on evidence and logical reasoning.

Narrative writing can have a variety of tones, depending on the story being told. It may incorporate dialogue, character development, and narrative techniques to engage the reader and create a specific atmosphere or mood.

Descriptive writing often employs rich, sensory language to create a specific mood or atmosphere. It appeals to the reader's senses and emotions, using vivid adjectives, adverbs, and sensory details.

## Focus

Expository writing focuses on presenting information, explaining concepts, or analyzing a topic. It prioritizes clarity, objectivity, and providing factual evidence.

Narrative storytelling emphasizes capturing readers' attention through engaging characters, plots, and events. It may incorporate elements of dialogue and personal experiences to convey a story effectively.

Descriptive writing uses vivid and detailed descriptions to create a sensory experience for the reader. It aims to make the reader visualize and experience what is being described.

While these writing styles have their unique characteristics, they are not mutually exclusive, and writers often use a combination of techniques to achieve their desired effect.

The following foundational writing elements can help you tell your story and keep readers involved.

## Conflict

A compelling nonfiction story may have some form of conflict with which the reader can engage. This can be a personal struggle or a broader societal issue. Adversity is a form of competition that may be apparent in stories where the main character must overcome some problem. This includes many types of characterization.

## Character Development

In a nonfiction story, we can consider the book's focus as an active character. This does not mean it becomes a person. It means the subject takes on specific characteristics. Whatever type of story, it should feature well-developed and relatable characters with whom the reader can emotionally connect. The nonfiction story may not personify an individual but might explore a subject, theory, or controversial idea. It could even focus on a community or a social issue, revealing the character of that community through its culture, shaped by the members of that group. Once we establish the community as an active character, we can follow it through adversity and the conflicts it confronts. For instance, a hurricane strikes a close-knit community. What challenges does the community face collectively? How do the people within the community react?"

## Setting

The story's location should be well-described and help create a mood or atmosphere that adds to the overall narrative. The setting does not necessarily need to be a physical location. The scene might be the political, social, or psychological setting or environment surrounding the subject.

## Narrative Arc

A nonfiction story can have a clear narrative arc with a beginning, middle, and end. The story must build towards a climax and provide a sense of resolution. In an essay format, this is called a conclusion. There are many ways to structure a narrative. In fiction writing, many stories use a three-act structure. A nonfiction story can use a similar form to tell a story. A visual example of this technique can be seen in "MurderBall,"[1], an award-winning documentary film. Murder Ball is nonfiction and structured like an action/drama fiction film scripted in three acts. The rivalry between the two teams, the US players versus Joe Soares and the Canadians, gives us clear a protagonist and antagonist. Joe Soares's aggressive and often insensitive behavior makes him the person to dislike, although, toward the middle of the film, he does get some redeeming value when he attends his non-jock son's concert. Another, more subtle antagonist in the movie is the personal physical limitations the athletes must overcome to play this contact sport.

## Authenticity

The story must be authentic and grounded in real-life events. This means the author conducted thorough research and accurately portrayed the events and people involved in the story. Every attempt is made to verify facts and witness information.

---

1  https://jrmartinmedia.com/murderball/

## Emotion

A nonfiction story can be more compelling by incorporating natural emotional elements that resonate with the reader. This can be achieved through character development, vivid description, and personal anecdotes. Emotion is created by actual events and people involved in telling the story.

## Relevance

The story should relate to the reader's interests and concerns. This can be achieved by selecting topics that are timely and meaningful. Quoting sources that support the ideas presented will help the reader to accept the relevance of what is written.

## Language

The language used in a nonfiction story should be clear, concise, and engaging. The author strives to use vivid and descriptive language that draws the reader into the story. This must be done in a way that does not embellish or exaggerate events and information.

## Perspective

The author's point of view is evident throughout the story. This can be achieved through the author's tone, voice, and narrative style. Objective reality facts usually support the author's point of view. Objective reality is the idea that facts are either true or false. Controversial topics can use objective reality facts to show both sides of an issue. Contrary to some political rhetoric, there are no alternate facts – no gray areas in objective reality. Support information with verifiable facts. A compelling nonfiction story is well-structured, grounded in authenticity, and emotionally engaging for the reader. The author creates a relevant, meaningful, and thought-provoking account.

## Activity

Think about an idea or two for a nonfiction story you can write. Consider the criteria in this chapter. Make notes about the ideas without judgment. Write about possibilities. Out of these notes, you can develop a concept for your story. Once you have a vision, outline how you can tell the story. How will it begin? Where will it go, and what ideas will you explore? What issues or ideas do you want to resolve in the end? Who might be interested in reading this story? What will these people gain or learn from reading the story?

Example: Write an article for New Yorker Magazine about the experience of owning a pet in an urban environment. How does the following outline meet the criteria discussed in this chapter?

**Title:** "Furry Companions: The Ups and Downs of Pet Ownership in the Urban Environment."

### Introduction[2]

A **heartwarming** and unexpected phenomenon takes center stage in the fast-paced and vibrant **urban landscape**—the profound bond between **city dwellers and their beloved pets.** In this engaging New Yorker article, we embark on a delightful journey into **urban pet ownership's** endearing and humorous realm. From **heartwarming canine camaraderie** to **mischievous feline antics**, we explore the **joys and challenges of raising pets** amidst the bustling realities of city living. Join us as we uncover the **quirks, adventures, and unique experiences** of sharing our lives with **furry companions in the urban world.**

---

2 Note Bold Italics: Key SEO words in the Introduction are set in italics for reference. See Chapter Five for details on SEO writing.

## Urban Pet Quirks

Explore the unique quirks of owning pets in the city—the struggle of finding pet-friendly apartments, the delicate balance of navigating busy streets during walks, and the amusing encounters with other urban pet parents. With urbane wit, we delve into the triumphs and tribulations of raising furry friends amidst skyscrapers and concrete.

## The Coffee Shop Cat Empire

Discover the clandestine society of cats that reside in the neighborhood's local coffee shops. Meet the feline overlords who reign over cappuccinos and lattes, captivating baristas and customers alike. Explore how these café cats bring warmth and delight to city life.

## The Peculiar Pet Groomers

Uncover the city's eccentric world of pet grooming services, where fluffy companions receive avant-garde haircuts and stylish make-overs. We interview pet owners who embrace the trend, turning their pets into mini-fashion icons, ready to strut their stuff down the streets of Manhattan.

## Introducing the Canine Commuters

Introduce readers to the elite group of dogs who have mastered the art of commuting with their owners. Witness the daily routine of these four-legged professionals as they navigate subway stations, boarding taxis, and even learning to hail Ubers—all with a wagging tail and an air of sophistication.

## Pet Cafés

Step into pet cafés, where the love for animals meets the culinary passions of the city's most talented chefs. From cat-themed pastries to "puppuccinos," we explore how these cafés serve delectable delights while celebrating the bond between humans and animals.

## Pets as Social Catalysts

Examine the role pets play in fostering social connections among urban residents. Whether it's striking up conversations at the dog park or joining dog-walking groups, we explore how pets become the bridge that connects people in this bustling metropolis.

## Pet Therapy in the Concrete Jungle

Delve into the heartwarming stories of pet-assisted therapy in the urban environment. From school therapy dogs to emotional support animals in offices, we shed light on pets' profound impact on mental well-being amidst the urban hustle.

### Conclusion

In this delightful journey through the world of urban pet ownership, we've seen how pets bring a touch of magic and whimsy to the daily lives of city dwellers. As we bid adieu to the quirky canines and fabulous felines, we leave with a renewed appreciation for the bonds forged between humans and their four-legged companions in the bustling heart of the concrete jungle.

31

## Target Audience

This New Yorker article is crafted for urban residents who share their lives with pets and appreciate the quirky humor that comes with city living. It also appeals to readers looking for heartwarming tales of human-animal connections amid the urban hustle.

## What Readers Will Gain

Readers will gain an insightful and entertaining peek into the urban pet owner's world, enriched with a touch of urbane humor. They'll discover the joys and challenges of pet ownership in the city and the undeniable bond between city dwellers and their furry companions.

*If I were pitching this article to a magazine editor, I might include some pictures in the article outline for illustration or if images could be used later.*

# CHAPTER 2

## Nonfiction Story Categories

## Part I

Nonfiction storytelling is the art of telling true stories in a way that engages and informs readers or viewers. It is a form of storytelling that uses narrative techniques to bring factual events and people to life and to connect with readers on a deeper emotional level. Nonfiction storytelling can take numerous forms and use any medium, including writing, film, video, audio, painting, exhibits, or theater. It can encompass themes from any domain, discipline, or topic. Nonfiction storytelling can be broadly categorized into diverse areas. In the first segment of this chapter, we'll elucidate these basic themes. In the second segment, we'll delve into various successful nonfiction books' structure and writing styles.

### Memoirs and Autobiographies

The main difference between a memoir and an autobiography lies in their scope and focus. A memoir is a form of autobiographical writing that focuses on specific events, experiences, or themes from the author's life. It typically centers around a particular period, relationship, or theme and delves into the author's reflections, emotions, and insights. Memoirs often employ narrative storytelling techniques to engage the reader and convey a sense of the author's subjective experience. They may selectively highlight critical moments or aspects of the author's life, providing a deeper exploration of their journey.

An autobiography is a more comprehensive and chronological account of a person's life, from birth to the present or at a specific time. Autobiographies strive to provide a complete and objective record of the author's life, covering various aspects such as childhood, education, career, relationships, and achievements. They often focus on factual details, historical context, and significant events without delving too deeply into personal reflections or interpretations. Autobiographies aim to present a comprehensive and accurate narrative of the author's life, often following a linear, chronological structure.

Memoirs and autobiographies share the goal of recounting an individual's life story. Memoirs focus on specific moments or themes, offering personal insights and emotions. Autobiographies provide a broader account of an individual's life.

**"Educated"** (2018) by Tara Westover is a powerful memoir that chronicles the author's journey from growing up in a strict and isolated household in rural Idaho to pursuing an education that ultimately transforms her life. Born into a family of survivalists who mistrusted the government and formal education, Westover's upbringing was marked by physical labor, harsh conditions, and the suppression of knowledge.

Despite her obstacles, Westover's thirst for knowledge led her to teach herself how to read, opening a new world of possibilities. As she grew older, her desire for education grew stronger, prompting her to seek admission to Brigham Young University. This decision meant navigating the challenges of leaving her family behind and confronting the conflicting ideals of her upbringing.

Through her compelling storytelling, Westover takes readers on a remarkable journey of self-discovery and resilience. She vividly portrays the tensions between her loyalty to her family, her pursuit of education, and the personal and intellectual growth she experiences. "Educated" is a compelling and inspiring memoir that explores themes of identity, education, and the power of knowledge to liberate and transform lives.

**"Life,"** by Keith Richards (2010). A personal account of the author's life experiences. Biographies and autobiographies often focus on a particular theme or period in the author's life and can offer insights into their personality, beliefs, and experiences. "Life" by Keith Richards is an autobiography written in the first person. It reads like he is talking directly to the reader with his London accent. It also includes childhood pictures of him, his family, the Rolling Stones, and others. Keith was aided in writing "Life" by James Fox, a journalist, and friend of Richards since the 1970s.

### Biographies

A detailed exploration and account of another person's life. Biographies often cover the subject's life and focus on their achievements, challenges, and impact on the world. This person could be known to the author, a historical figure, or a contemporary person. The biographer lets the reader know what makes this person's life important for others to know about.

**"Steve Jobs"** by Walter Isaacson – a biography published in 2011, tells the story of the life and career of Steve Jobs, cofounder of Apple Inc. Isaacson uses narrative techniques to explore Jobs' personality, successes and failures, and impact on the technology industry. Walter Isaacson's writing style in "Steve Jobs" can be described as comprehensive, journalistic, and narrative-driven. Isaacson employs extensive research, interviews, and storytelling techniques to present a detailed and intimate portrait of Steve Jobs, Apple Inc.'s cofounder.

Isaacson's writing style is characterized by its attention to detail and ability to weave together various aspects of Jobs' life, including his personal relationships, career achievements, and the innovative products he helped create. The book incorporates interviews with Jobs and his colleagues, friends, and family, providing multiple perspectives on his life and work.

The author's journalistic approach thoroughly explores Jobs' character, strengths, and flaws. Isaacson delves into the complexities of Jobs' personality, including his visionary mindset, relentless pursuit of perfection, and sometimes abrasive interpersonal style. Through vivid storytelling, Isaacson captures the key moments and challenges in Jobs' life, painting a compelling and nuanced portrait of this influential figure.

Isaacson's writing style in "Steve Jobs" combines meticulous research, journalistic rigor, and narrative flair to present a comprehensive and engaging account of Steve Jobs' life and impact on the technology industry.

## Historical Nonfiction

Storytelling in this category focuses on historical events and periods, providing a factual account of past events. History books may include primary source documents, interviews, and research from multiple sources. The story can go beyond events and dates and look at the people involved. While adhering to nonfiction standards, historical writing reflects the writer's subjective interpretation. Even if they witness the history they are writing about, they see it through their eyes, experiences, and cultures. The history of civilization is written by the survivors, winners of wars and events. It is essential and critical for writers to examine their research, opinions, and conclusions from many standpoints.

**"Silk Roads – A New History of the World,"** Peter Frankopan, 2015 is an internationally acclaimed nonfiction book that effectively employs historical analysis to weave a compelling narrative about the impact of the Silk Roads on global history. Frankopan's writing style is engaging and detailed, artfully combining anecdotal storytelling with scholarly research to bring the past to life.

The author presents an exhaustive account of the Silk Roads, the ancient trade routes that stretched from the Middle East through the steppe and South Asia to China. The book's narrative is rigorously supported by factual information, underlining the author's commitment to historical accuracy. He provides ample evidence to support his claims, often citing primary sources and drawing on an extensive range of secondary materials, including archaeological findings, texts, and historiographical interpretations. The book is well-documented, demonstrating the author's ability to verify information and challenge pre-existing notions.

The characterization in this work of historical nonfiction is superb. Rather than presenting the societies, cities, and empires along the Silk Roads as monolithic entities, Frankopan infuses them with individual characteristics, motivations, and responses to different historical circumstances. His deep dive into the civilizations of the East and West offers an intimate portrayal of their histories, cultures, and religions, from the rise and fall of empires to the advent of Buddhism, Christianity, and Islam.

The author's eastward reorientation of global history destabilizes conventional Eurocentric perspectives and highlights the intrinsic interconnectedness of East and West, a defining feature of this book. Through the lens of the Silk Roads, Frankopan challenges readers to reconsider the origins of contemporary geopolitical and economic phenomena. The book's underlying theme is the world's intricate interdependence and how the West's fate has always been intimately tied to the East.

Ultimately, "Silk Roads: A New History of the World" not only provides an insightful exploration of the Silk Roads' historical significance but also uses these ancient trade routes as a metaphor for global interconnectedness, shedding light on the present and future implications of the world's past interactions. This engaging piece of historical nonfiction offers a broad, integrative view of world history that challenges traditional Western-centered paradigms.

### Investigative Journalism

An in-depth examination of a specific topic or issue. Investigative journalism often involves interviews, research, and primary source documents to uncover new information and present a detailed and factual account of the subject.

**"Bad Blood: Secrets and Lies in a Silicon Valley Startup"** is an exceptional work of investigative journalism written by journalist John Carreyrou.  Beginning in 2015, he wrote a series of stories for The Wall Street Journal on the subject. In 2018 he published "Bad Blood," a best-selling book on the hoax. The book presents a riveting and shocking exposé of Theranos. This once-celebrated healthcare technology company promised revolutionary blood testing capabilities but ultimately turned out to be built on deception and fraud.

Carreyrou takes readers on a captivating journey through the rise and fall of Theranos, led by its charismatic founder, Elizabeth Holmes. With meticulous research and firsthand interviews, the author unravels the layers of deception that permeated the company's operations, revealing a web of lies, manipulation, and ethical violations.

The story follows Carreyrou's investigation as he unravels the truth behind Theranos' claims of revolutionizing the medical industry. Through interviews with former employees, industry experts, and whistleblowers, he uncovers a culture of secrecy, bullying, and scientific incompetence that persisted within the company. Carreyrou's relentless pursuit of the truth brings to light the fraudulent practices employed by Theranos, where faulty technology and inaccurate test results endangered patients' lives.

Carreyrou explores connections between Theranos and influential figures in politics and business, highlighting the allure and power of Silicon Valley's startup culture. The author sheds light on the complicity of high-profile individuals who supported and invested in the company without thoroughly examining its claims.

Published in 2018, "Bad Blood" received widespread acclaim for its gripping storytelling and meticulous investigative reporting. It offers readers an in-depth understanding of the Theranos scandal, revealing the darker side of Silicon Valley's startup ecosystem and emphasizing the critical role of investigative journalism in holding powerful entities accountable.

Disgraced Elizabeth Holmes surrendered to federal prison on May 30, 2023, to begin serving an eleven-year term for defrauding investors.

### Science and Nature Nonfiction

Storytelling in this category focuses on scientific discoveries and natural phenomena. These books may cover many topics, including physics, biology, astronomy, environmental science, and other disciplines.

Successful nonfiction writing in children's books often embodies the following attributes:

**Accessibility:** The language should be age-appropriate and understandable for the intended audience. Complex concepts should be simplified and explained in ways children can relate to and comprehend.

**Engaging Narrative:** Unlike textbooks, successful nonfiction children's books often incorporate storytelling elements. They might present information through an interesting narrative or a compelling sequence of events.

**Visual Appeal:** Children's nonfiction often includes vibrant, attractive illustrations or photographs. Visuals can help children understand and remember information more effectively.

**Interactivity**: Features such as questions, quizzes, hands-on experiments, or activities can increase engagement and help children to learn and absorb the presented information actively.

**Relevance:** Topics that interest children should be selected or related to their everyday experiences. The more relevant the subject matter, the more engaged the young readers will likely be.

**Accuracy:** While the content should be simplified for children, it's crucial to maintain factual accuracy. The information should be thoroughly researched and verified from reliable sources.

**Inclusion of Fascinating Facts:** Children love learning unusual or surprising facts. Including these can spark curiosity and make the learning experience fun and exciting.

**Clear Structure:** The information should be organized clearly and logically. This might mean dividing the book into sections or chapters, using headings and subheadings, or creating a timeline or step-by-step process.

**Inspirational and Educational:** The content should inspire children to learn more, cultivate a love for reading, and ignite their curiosity about the world.

**Diversity and Representation**: In today's globalized world, children's nonfiction must include diverse perspectives and voices, allowing them to see themselves and others in their books.

**"The Fascinating Science Book for Kids: 500 Stupendous Science Facts 2020,"** by Kevin Kurtz MA, is an engaging piece of science nonfiction geared towards children aged 9 to 12. It successfully aligns with the criteria for science nonfiction writing, incorporating an array of captivating scientific information across various topics, from dinosaurs and deep-sea creatures to celestial bodies and the intricacies of the human body. There is a large market for nonfiction written for children.

*"The Fascinating Science Book for Kids"* makes science accessible and exciting for young readers, a crucial characteristic of compelling science nonfiction. It emphasizes fact-based content, promising to deliver 500 "stupendous" science facts. These facts, such as the mention of tiny diamonds falling from the sky on Neptune, the unusual brain shape of the giant squid, or the electric-generating bacteria species, offer verifiable scientific information in a digestible format and stimulate curiosity and wonder in young minds.

One of the features of this book is its effective use of full-color illustrations on every page, which aids in the communication of scientific facts and engages readers on a visual level. The images serve a dual purpose. They provide visual representations of the subjects being discussed and offer a means of capturing and maintaining the interest of the target age group. By combining accurate textual information with vivid and engaging illustrations, the book fosters a better understanding of scientific concepts and processes among young readers.

This book focuses on exotic and far-reaching topics such as prehistoric life and outer space. Still, it highlights science in everyday environments like the readers' backyards. This approach makes science relatable and applicable to the readers' daily lives, a valuable aspect of effective science nonfiction writing.

"The Fascinating Science Book for Kids: 500 Stupendous Science Facts" successfully combines a comprehensive array of intriguing and verifiable scientific facts with visually appealing illustrations, making it both an educational and enjoyable reading experience for young science enthusiasts.

## Textbooks

Textbook writing, particularly for complex scientific subjects such as quantum mechanics, necessitates adherence to several crucial criteria. A textbook should be accurate and reliable: Given that the primary purpose of textbooks is to educate, they should provide accurate and up-to-date information. Facts, theories, and interpretations must be consistent with the academic community's current understanding.

**Be clear and organized:** Textbooks must be logically structured with clear learning objectives, subheadings, summaries, and end-of-chapter reviews. This helps students understand the progression of topics and makes the material more manageable.

**Engage with the reader:** The writing style must draw the reader into the subject matter. A dry or overly complicated writing style may discourage learners, whereas a more accessible and engaging approach can inspire them.

**Provide context:** Textbooks present facts and explain their relevance and context. This might involve discussing the historical development of a concept or its real-world applications.

**Include supplementary material:** Useful illustrations, diagrams, examples, exercises, and problem sets can significantly enhance the learning experience.

**Encourage critical thinking**: Instead of merely conveying information, a good textbook will challenge students to engage with the material, draw their conclusions, and think critically about the subject matter.

**"Introduction to Quantum Mechanics 3rd Edition,"** 2019 by David J. Griffiths and Darrell F. Schroeter is an excellent example of a textbook that meets these criteria.

Firstly, the book is commended for its accuracy and reliability, adhering strictly to established principles and theories of quantum mechanics. It remains current, reflecting advancements in the field in its 3rd edition.

The textbook is well-structured and logically organized, starting with the fundamental concepts and progressively moving to more complex topics. This helps students build on their knowledge systematically. Clear objectives are set at the beginning of each chapter, and key points are summarized at the end.

The authors have a conversational and approachable writing style, which helps make a challenging subject like quantum mechanics more accessible to readers. They do not shy away from injecting humor into the text, which can keep readers engaged and alleviate the intimidation factor of the subject.

The book does an excellent job of providing context. It elucidates the historical development of quantum mechanics and discusses the philosophical implications of the theory, thereby highlighting its significance beyond the realm of pure science.

Supplementary material is another strong point of this textbook. It features precise, illustrative diagrams and many examples, exercises, and problem sets. These are integral in helping students apply and practice what they have learned.

The authors frequently encourage critical thinking by challenging readers to tackle difficult questions and paradoxes within quantum mechanics. This approach pushes students to engage more deeply with the material and develop problem-solving skills.

## Travel

Personal or researched accounts of a particular place or travel experience. Travel writing often includes local culture, history, and environment descriptions. Most travel books written as guides include pictures of the destination. Illustrations, maps, and tours are suggested.

**"I Never Knew That About Ireland,"** Christopher Winn, 2016, exemplifies the genre of nonfiction travel literature through its engaging exploration of the lesser-known aspects of Irish history and culture. It encapsulates a journey through Ireland's four provinces, bringing to light myths, legends, inventions, and adventures that define the nation's historical landscape.

Nonfiction travel writing needs to effectively capture and convey the essence of a place, from its physical landscape and historical significance to its cultural nuances and local anecdotes. This book does so with aplomb. It provides factual information about Ireland's provinces and beyond to introduce the reader to unique trivia, myths, and legends, effectively transporting readers to the heart of the Irish experience.

One criterion of travel nonfiction is providing vivid, evocative descriptions of locations, which this book does successfully. For instance, it introduces readers to places like the holy mountain Croagh Patrick, the burial chamber at Newgrange, and Lismore Castle, each presented with unique and captivating details.

The book demonstrates a deep understanding of Irish culture, further immersing readers in the country's unique environment. By covering subjects as diverse as religious history, architectural achievements, and even Ireland's influence on global brands like Coca-Cola, the book provides an expansive look into the country's influence locally and globally.

Another essential criterion this book meets is its ability to engage readers, stirring their curiosity and offering them an educational and entertaining experience. The text is written in an engaging and accessible style, incorporating exciting trivia and anecdotes that will surprise and delight readers.

This book is a valuable guide and companion for travelers, as good travel nonfiction should. Whether readers are planning an Irish vacation, reminiscing about past visits, or dreaming of experiencing Ireland, this book provides an enriching journey through Ireland's historical and cultural landscape.

"*I Never Knew That About Ireland*" embodies the core criteria of nonfiction travel writing, offering an engaging, informative, and immersive journey through the lesser-known facets of Irish history and culture.

## Essay and Short Nonfiction Stories

A personal reflection on a particular topic or issue. Essays may cover various topics, from politics and culture to personal experiences and emotions. Typically, an essay contains an introduction, body paragraphs, and a conclusion. The opening may include a hook, context, and a thesis statement that presents the main argument. Body paragraphs include supporting evidence, examples, and data to support the main idea—also, analysis and explanation of the evidence demonstrating its relevance to the thesis. The conclusion should include a restatement of the thesis and a summary of the main points discussed in the essay. Include closing thoughts or final insights related to the topic. Concluding statements must leave a lasting impression on the reader.

The number of body paragraphs can vary depending on the length and complexity of the essay. Each body paragraph should focus on a central idea or argument and present supporting evidence. Additionally, the order of the body paragraphs can vary depending on the logic or flow of your views.

In addition to the structural elements, it's essential to ensure coherence and cohesion throughout the essay. This can be achieved using transitional words and phrases to guide the reader through the different sections and ideas of the essay. Essays are often written as articles for magazines. In this case, the structure may resemble a short story.

**A few examples listed in "Top Ten Essays Since 1950" Robert Atwan, Publisher's Weekly.**

### James Baldwin's "Notes of a Native Son." 1955, Harper's.

"Notes of a Native Son" by James Baldwin: A seminal piece in American literature, Baldwin's essay explores the intricate relationship between race and identity in mid-20th century America. Written against the backdrop of his father's death and the 1943 Harlem Riots, Baldwin delves into his personal experiences and reflections, juxtaposing his father's bitterness towards white society with his own evolving understanding of racial dynamics, ultimately leading to a profound epiphany about love and hate.

### John McPhee's "The Search for Marvin Gardens." 1972, The New Yorker.

"The Search for Marvin Gardens" by John McPhee: An innovative blend of game narration and social commentary, McPhee's essay uses the Monopoly board game as a metaphor to examine American urban decay. As the game progresses, McPhee interweaves the narrative with descriptions of the real-life Atlantic City neighborhoods, illuminating the disparity between the game's idyllic representation and the gritty realities of urban life in America.

### Annie Dillard's "Total Eclipse." Antaeus, 1982.

This intense and dramatic narrative captures Dillard's total solar eclipse experience. More than a scientific observation, the essay delves into the existential dread and awe that this celestial event evokes. Dillard's vivid descriptions create a surreal, almost apocalyptic atmosphere that reflects on the impermanence of life and the humbling power of nature.

### "Consider the Lobster." 2004, Gourmet.

*"Consider the Lobster"* by David Foster Wallace originally intended to review the Maine Lobster Festival. Wallace's essay transforms into an ethical inquiry about animal suffering and the nature of gourmet food festivals. Wallace's incisive commentary and philosophical musings pose uncomfortable questions about the morality of boiling lobsters alive for human consumption, making readers reconsider their culinary choices and cultural practices.

### Jo Ann Beard, "The Fourth State of Matter." 1996, The New Yorker.

A deeply personal and poignant account of a tragic event, Beard's essay chronicles her experiences leading up to and following a mass shooting at the University of Iowa, where she worked. Intertwining the mundanities of her daily life with the ensuing horror, Beard paints a vivid picture of grief, trauma, and survival, providing a profound exploration of the human capacity to endure adversity.

### Self-help and Personal Development

Advice and guidance on personal growth and development. Self-help books often focus on relationships, career development, and physical and mental health. This category is vast, with advice on everything from winning friends to dog grooming. Here are a few examples of Top selling Self-help books.

**"How to Win Friends and Influence People" (1936) by Dale Carnegie:** This pioneering work in the self-help genre stands out for its conversational style and accessibility.

Carnegie's voice is friendly and encouraging, treating the reader as a confidante. He draws on numerous anecdotes and real-life stories to deliver his lessons, making his advice relatable and practical. The book's central theme emphasizes empathy and genuine interest in others as critical strategies to influence people and create meaningful relationships.

**"The 7 Habits of Highly Effective People"** (1989) by Stephen R. Covey: Covey's authoritative and persuasive voice imparts a deep sense of wisdom throughout the book. He employs a logical, sequential style that guides readers through a transformational journey from dependence to independence and interdependence. The book offers an integrative framework for personal and professional effectiveness, and its didactic voice emphasizes the timeless nature of principles like proactive initiative, prioritization, and synergistic collaboration.

**"Atomic Habits: An Easy & Proven Way to Build Good Habits & Break Bad Ones"** (2018) by James Clear: Clear's book is characterized by its clear, crisp, and direct writing style. His voice is instructive, offering actionable advice backed by scientific research. The book effectively translates complex theories into easy-to-understand concepts with plenty of real-life examples and practical strategies. Its central theme focuses on the cumulative power of small, incremental changes—atomic habits—in achieving significant results over time.

**"The Four Agreements: A Practical Guide to Personal Freedom,"** (1977) by Don Miguel Ruiz: Don Miguel Ruiz's writing style is poetic, philosophical, and full of symbolic imagery. The book draws on ancient Toltec wisdom, and Ruiz's voice carries a spiritual and mystic tone. The four agreements - be impeccable with your word, don't take anything personally, don't make assumptions, and always do your best - are delivered as simple but profound truths for personal liberation. The book emphasizes introspection and emotional self-awareness for a path to freedom.

### True crime

This type of nonfiction storytelling focuses on real-life crimes and investigations. Actual crime books may include interviews with investigators, witnesses, and perpetrators and detailed descriptions of the crime and investigation process.

A few best-selling examples according to Barnes and Noble Books.

**"The Art Thief, A True Story of Love, Crime, and a Dangerous Obsession"** (2023) by Michael Finkel: In "The Art Thief," Finkel employs an engaging and investigative narrative style. His writing, enriched with intricate detail and depth, transforms the factual accounts into a compelling storyline. His voice is reflective and empathetic, adding a human dimension to the story and exploring the motivations and obsessions of the art thief. The book takes readers on an exhilarating ride through the world of fine art, unearthing the dangerous habits that drive art theft.

**"Killers of the Flower Moon, The Osage Murders, and the Birth of the FBI"** (2018) by David Grann. Grann's work exemplifies immersive journalism; his voice is composed yet impassioned, and his storytelling is evocative. He weaves historical facts with personal narratives, creating an engaging and chilling account of greed and prejudice in 1920s America. The book unveils the systematic murders of wealthy Osage Native Americans after they discovered oil under their land, marking a pivotal moment in the evolution of the FBI.

**"In Cold Blood: A True Account of a Multiple Murder and its Consequences"** (1994) by Truman Capote: As a pioneering work in the true crime genre, "In Cold Blood" stands out for its novelistic style, blending fact with fiction-like narrative. Capote's voice is calm, analytical yet eerily intimate. He meticulously recounts the brutal murder of the Clutter family in Kansas and the subsequent investigation, revealing the factual details and the psychological depth of the killers. This masterpiece is often seen as a touchstone for narrative nonfiction and is acclaimed for exploring the American psyche and the nature of evil.

## Business and Finance

Nonfiction storytelling in this category focuses on business and finance topics, including entrepreneurship, investing, and personal finance. These books often provide practical advice and strategies for success in these areas. Many Business and Finance nonfiction books are listed in multiple categories.

**"Rich Dad, Poor Dad"** (1997) by Robert T. Kiyosaki. Kiyosaki's writing style is straightforward and conversational, employing anecdotes from his life to convey financial education concepts. His voice is both motivational and instructive. The book uses the contrast between his "rich dad" (his friend's financially knowledgeable father) and "poor dad" (his own well-educated but financially illiterate father) to highlight the importance of financial literacy.

**"*The Intelligent Investor*"** (1949) by Benjamin Graham: Considered a bible of value investing, Graham's work has an authoritative, academic style. His voice is pragmatic and didactic, emphasizing a disciplined approach to investing. The book provides profound insights into various investment principles, promoting the idea of 'investing in the business' rather than 'speculating in stocks.'

**"Think and Grow Rich"** (1937) by Napoleon Hill: Hill employs a persuasive and motivational style in this seminal work, offering a blend of self-help and business wisdom. His voice is encouraging and confident, stemming from his extensive research of successful individuals. He presents the concept of harnessing one's desires and thoughts to attain financial success, offering principles based on his Law of Success philosophy.

**"The Psychology of Money"** (2020) by Morgan Housel. Housel's writing style is engaging, insightful, and highly accessible, highlighting managing money's emotional and psychological aspects. His voice is thoughtful and introspective, offering personal stories and historical examples to convey finance's often overlooked but crucial elements, including saving, investing, and behavioral economics.

**"Shoe Dog: A Memoir by the Creator of Nike"** (2016) by Phil Knight. Knight adopts a candid, narrative style, detailing his entrepreneurial journey with authenticity and passion. His voice is introspective and resilient, taking the readers on an intimate journey of Nike's creation and growth. The memoir provides an unfiltered view of the challenges and triumphs of building a global brand.

**"Freakonomics: A Rogue Economist Explores the Hidden Side of Everything"** (2005) by Steven D. Levitt and Stephen J. Dubner. Levitt and Dubner's writing is innovative and provocative, employing economic theory to explore unusual real-world phenomena. Their voice is curious and irreverent, questioning conventional wisdom and revealing hidden truths in unexpected places. The book applies economic concepts to diverse subjects like crime rates, parenting, and cheating, showing the surprising economics behind everyday life.

# Part 2

## Nonfiction Storytelling Requirements

Real people and events. Nonfiction storytelling is grounded in real people, events, and ideas. The writing seeks to convey objective information to the reader or viewer. Nonfiction storytelling may have a stated point of view but should use facts and objective reality to establish a subjective perspective.

At the heart of nonfiction storytelling lies the foundation of real people, events, and ideas. Unlike fiction, which springs from the imagination, nonfiction is rooted in the tangible world, drawing inspiration from the rich tapestry of human experiences and environmental events. Nonfiction writing aims to present objective information to the reader or viewer, offering a window into the truths and realities that shape our lives.

While nonfiction storytelling may have a stated point of view, it maintains a commitment to using facts and objective reality as its cornerstones. Through meticulous research, interviews, and firsthand accounts, nonfiction writers strive to uncover and present the truth in a compelling narrative. Drawing from reliable sources, empirical evidence, and verifiable data establishes a strong foundation of credibility that fosters trust and engages the audience.

However, within this objective framework, nonfiction storytelling also embraces the subjective perspective of the writer. While facts are the building blocks, they are skillfully woven to create a narrative that carries the writer's unique voice and interpretation. By infusing personal insights, reflections, and analysis, the writer adds depth and meaning to the objective information, allowing the audience to connect with the story more profoundly.

In essence, nonfiction storytelling seeks to strike a delicate balance between objectivity and subjectivity. It harnesses the power of facts and objective reality to establish a robust and reliable framework while embracing the subjective lens through which the writer perceives and interprets the world. This combination of factual information and subjective perspective allows nonfiction storytelling to convey not only the what and the how but also the why, providing a nuanced understanding of the complex and multifaceted nature of the human experience.

## "I Know Why the Caged Bird Sings" by Maya Angelou, 1969

Maya Angelou's "I Know Why the Caged Bird Sings" is a remarkable autobiography that weaves a poignant narrative about her early years. This book effectively embodies the hallmarks of nonfiction writing, incorporating accurate personal experiences, exploring profound themes, and presenting an engaging narrative that is both educational and emotive.

Angelou's writing style is characterized by its eloquence and vividness. Her ability to craft strikingly vivid imagery and emotionally charged descriptions sets her apart. Angelou's prose is poetic, reflecting her talent as a poet and as a performer. She expertly employs metaphors, similes, and other literary devices to convey the nuances of her experiences. Her writing is also candid and unflinchingly honest, unafraid to delve into the challenging aspects of her past, contributing to her autobiography's raw emotional impact.

While "*I Know Why the Caged Bird Sings*" follows a chronological structure tracing Angelou's life from childhood to teenage years, the book stands out for its thematic development. Rather than just recounting events, Angelou explores profound themes such as racism, identity, self-acceptance, resilience, and freedom, which give the book depth and universal relevance.

The theme of self-acceptance is particularly prominent. Throughout the narrative, Angelou grapples with feelings of displacement, marginalization, and a struggle for self-acceptance, mainly because of her race and the trauma she experiences. The "caged bird" in the title serves as a metaphor for her confinement due to societal prejudices and personal trials. Angelou's journey to self-acceptance is a transformative process, where she learns to embrace her identity, overcome her traumas, and discover her self-worth.

One pivotal scene illustrating the self-acceptance theme occurs when Angelou, after reading a book by a black author, realizes that black girls like her can be intelligent and creative. This catalyzes a crucial shift in her self-perception, leading to greater self-acceptance and self-confidence.

"*I Know Why the Caged Bird Sings*" is a powerful exploration of self-discovery and personal resilience. Through Angelou's richly detailed narrative and profound thematic development, the book provides readers with an in-depth understanding of her experiences and insights, making it a compelling piece of nonfiction writing.

"*I Know Why the Caged Bird Sings* liberates the reader into life simply because Maya Angelou confronts her own life with such a moving wonder, such a luminous dignity."—James Baldwin.

## Narrative Structure and Balance

Imagine a nonfiction story unfolding before your eyes, with characters that come to life through their actions and experiences. In this narrative journey, character development takes center stage as we delve into the minds and hearts of real individuals who shape events. Whether it's a historical account or a contemporary tale, nonfiction writing strives to portray these characters' thoughts, feelings, and motivations in a way that captivates and resonates with the audience. The characters become the driving force behind the narrative. We witness their growth, challenges, and transformations, much like the protagonists in fiction. Their stories unfold in a clear beginning, middle, and end, weaving a captivating arc that engages readers or viewers. We become invested in their journeys, rooting for their success, empathizing with their struggles, and celebrating their triumphs.

In nonfiction, a single moment in time can take on the role of a central character, anchoring the story and driving its momentum. It could be a defining historical event, like the signing of a peace treaty or the eruption of a volcano. The protagonist and antagonist may manifest as two factions locked in a fierce conflict, whether a war, a political struggle, or a battle for social justice. By portraying these characters and their roles within the larger narrative, nonfiction writing breathes life into the past, sheds light on the present, and even illuminates potential futures.

Nonfiction character development focuses beyond mere information and facts. It seeks to create an emotional connection with the readers or viewers, allowing them to experience the story more deeply. By understanding and conveying real people's thoughts, feelings, and motivations, nonfiction writing can inspire, educate, and provoke meaningful reflections about the human experience. It invites us to see the world through their eyes and empathize with their joys and sorrows, ultimately reminding us of our shared humanity.

However, writing news for a newspaper or television news show requires adherence to strict journalism practices and formats. It is pure nonfiction with as little subjective interpretation as possible. The Associated Press Stylebook is a guide for news writing. According to Wikipedia, **"The Associated Press Stylebook,"** alternatively titled *"The Associated Press Stylebook and Briefing on Media Law,"* is a style and usage guide for American English grammar created by American journalists working for or connected with the Associated Press journalism cooperative based in New York City."

## Verifiable sources

Nonfiction stories rely on verifiable sources and evidence to support their claims and convey accurate information to the audience. Here are a few examples of nonfiction stories that depend on verifiable sources and evidence to support their claims:

**"Sapiens: A Brief History of Humankind"** by Yuval Noah Harari: This book explores the history of human evolution and civilization, drawing on a wide range of archaeological, anthropological, and historical sources to present a comprehensive and evidence-based account of our species' journey.

**"The Immortal Life of Henrietta Lacks"** by Rebecca Skloot: This nonfiction work tells the story of Henrietta Lacks, a woman whose cells were used without her knowledge or consent for scientific research. The author meticulously researched and interviewed family members, scientists, and medical records to present a compelling narrative that sheds light on ethical issues in medical science.

**"The Devil in the White City"** by Erik Larson intertwines the true stories of two men: the architect behind the 1893 Chicago World's Fair and a serial killer operating simultaneously. Larson extensively researched newspaper articles, court records, and historical documents to reconstruct the events and provide a captivating account of the fair and the crimes.

The above examples demonstrate how nonfiction stories rely on verifiable sources and evidence to ensure accuracy and credibility. Drawing upon well-documented facts, interviews, and research, these authors present narratives grounded in reality and supported by a wealth of information.

## Theme and Message

Nonfiction stories often strive to convey a larger truth or insight about the world through a central theme or message. While they present factual information, they also aim to resonate with the reader or viewer on a deeper level, evoking emotions, sparking reflection, or prompting a change in perspective.

## Connection to the reader/viewer

Nonfiction stories engage the audience by tapping into universal experiences, emotions, or struggles. They explore relatable themes such as love, loss, resilience, justice, or personal growth, which resonate with readers or viewers and create a sense of shared humanity.

## Exploration of Complex Issues

Nonfiction stories often tackle complex social, political, or cultural issues to shed light on different perspectives and encourage critical thinking. Presenting a theme or message invites readers or viewers to consider the implications and explore their beliefs and values.

## Emotional Impact

Nonfiction stories have the power to evoke strong emotions in the audience. They can provoke empathy, outrage, inspiration, or admiration through the stories of real people and their experiences. By delving into personal narratives, nonfiction stories connect emotionally, leaving a lasting impact on the audience.

### Seeking Deeper Truths

While nonfiction stories are grounded in facts, they may go beyond surface details to uncover deeper truths about the human condition or our world. They strive to illuminate hidden dynamics, expose injustices, challenge prevailing narratives, or provide insight into the complexities of our society.

Overall, nonfiction stories aim to go beyond the mere presentation of facts and engage the reader or viewer on a deeper level. They offer an opportunity to explore profound themes, spark contemplation, and convey a larger truth or insight that resonates with the audience long after the story has been told.

# Part 3

# Compelling Nonfiction Storytelling

We've looked at broad categories of nonfiction. In this section, we'll more closely examine work that reached a large audience and has stood the test of time. There are also examples of covers of several books.

In 1959, Truman Capote, a novelist, and his friend Harper Lee (who would later become the author of "*To Kill a Mockingbird*") arrived in Holcomb, Kansas. Capote's purpose was to investigate the brutal murder of the Clutter family, which appeared to be a random act of violence. He intended to interview extended family, friends, and investigators in the isolated town in Kansas's wheat-growing region. Over the course of six years, Capote dedicated himself to writing what he referred to as a "nonfiction novel." This work was published as a four-part crime series in The New Yorker in 1965.

Truman Capote's **"In Cold Blood"** is a story that uses narrative techniques to bring the events and people to life and explores the killers' motivations and psychology. It falls under the "True Crime" category. Truman Capote's *In Cold Blood* is a remarkable example of a true crime story that masterfully employs narrative techniques to immerse readers in a chilling and gripping tale. Blurring the boundaries between fiction and nonfiction, Capote meticulously reconstructs the real-life events surrounding the brutal murders of the Clutter family in Holcomb, Kansas. Through his meticulous research and interviews with the perpetrators, Perry Smith and Richard Hickock, Capote weaves a compelling narrative that delves into their motivations and psychology.

By adopting a narrative approach, Capote breathes life into the characters and events, allowing readers to intimately experience the harrowing moments of the crime and its aftermath. He skillfully captures the essence of the Clutter family, providing glimpses into their lives, dreams, and aspirations, which makes their tragic fate all the more poignant. Simultaneously, Capote dives into the minds of Smith and Hickock, exploring their troubled backgrounds, complex personalities, and the factors that ultimately led them down a path of violence.

Capote constructs a narrative beyond the mere chronicle of a crime through careful attention to detail and a keen eye for storytelling. He captures the atmosphere of the small town, the tension in the community, and the impact of the murders on the collective psyche. Capote's vivid descriptions, dialogue, and narrative structure draw readers into the story, enabling them to comprehend the intricate web of events and the profound implications of the crime.

"*In Cold Blood*" epitomizes the true crime genre, offering a compelling blend of factual reporting and narrative storytelling. It goes beyond merely presenting facts and engages readers emotionally and intellectually. Capote's meticulous research, coupled with his narrative prowess, creates a work that sheds light on a heinous crime and explores the complexities of human nature, morality, and the elusive nature of truth.

### Essays and Nonfiction Short Stories

The essay or biographical short story **"My Family's Slave"** (2017) by Alex Tizon, published in The Atlantic Magazine, is a poignant and thought-provoking exploration of the author's family history and their complex relationship with Eudocia Tomas Pulido, a domestic worker who was essentially enslaved for decades. Tizon skillfully combines biographical and historical nonfiction elements to delve into the deeply personal and painful story that spans generations.

Structurally, the essay follows a chronological narrative, tracing the author's upbringing in the Philippines and the presence of Lola, as Eudocia was called, in his family's household. Tizon takes readers on a journey through his childhood memories, providing vivid descriptions and anecdotes highlighting the complexities of the relationship between his family and Lola. He interweaves these personal recollections with historical context, examining the broader social and cultural forces that perpetuated the system of domestic servitude in the Philippines.

The content of the essay is both introspective and investigative. Tizon reflects on his complicity and the moral implications of his family's treatment of Lola. He grapples with the conflicting emotions of love, guilt, and obligation that colored his perception of Lola and their shared experiences. Additionally, Tizon explores the broader historical and societal factors that allowed such a dehumanizing system to persist and examines the legacy of colonialism and power dynamics within Filipino society.

Throughout the essay, Tizon's prose is emotive and evocative, creating a deeply immersive experience for the reader. He combines vivid descriptions, powerful anecdotes, and introspective reflections to bring the characters and the historical context to life. The essay prompts readers to confront uncomfortable truths about power, privilege, and the exploitation of vulnerable individuals within family structures.

In summary, **"My Family's Slave"** is a remarkable essay that blends biographical and historical nonfiction to unravel a profoundly personal and unsettling story. Through its well-crafted structure and compelling content, Tizon invites readers to grapple with complex questions about power, morality, and the lasting impacts of systemic oppression.

### Historical Nonfiction Storytelling

In these titles, authors adopt an engaging and accessible writing style, making complex ideas and theories accessible to a broad audience. They combine meticulous research with storytelling techniques to present a compelling narrative that captivates readers and invites them to question traditional perspectives on human history.

**"The Warmth of Other Suns"** by Isabel Wilkerson - published in 2010- tells the story of the Great Migration, a mass movement of African Americans from the South to the North and West between 1915 and 1970. Wilkerson uses narrative techniques to bring the experiences of individual migrants to life, weaving together their stories to create a broader historical narrative.

**"In the Garden of Beasts"** by Erik Larson - published in 2011, this book tells the story of William E. Dodd, the first American ambassador to Nazi Germany, and his family's experiences in Berlin in the 1930s. Larson uses narrative techniques to bring the time's personalities and politics to life and explore the complex relationships between the United States and Nazi Germany. This approach to history is called "novelistic." It may not be purely historical nonfiction because of the hybrid style.

**"1491" by Charles C. Mann** - published in 2005, this book challenges traditional Western views of pre-Columbian America and tells the story of the civilizations that existed on the continent before European contact. Mann uses narrative techniques to explore the cultures and societies of these civilizations, bringing their achievements and tragedies to life.

**"The Dawn of Everything – A New History of Humanity"** (2022) by David Graeber and David Wengrow is a thought-provoking nonfiction book that challenges conventional narratives of human history. It explores the origins and evolution of human societies through an interdisciplinary lens, presenting a compelling case for reimagining our understanding of the past. It is nonfiction that combines history, anthropology, archaeology, and sociology. It presents arguments that contradict traditional thinking in these disciplines.

*"The Dawn of Everything"* draws upon various academic disciplines, like history, anthropology, and archaeology, to examine the foundations of human society. The authors analyze archaeological evidence, historical records, and anthropological studies to present a fresh perspective on the emergence of culture, politics, and social institutions. Their interdisciplinary approach encourages readers to critically engage with the subject matter and consider alternative interpretations of human history.

In *"The Dawn of Everything,"* Graeber and Wengrow challenge long-standing assumptions about human society, offering a thought-provoking exploration of our shared past. Through their accessible writing style and interdisciplinary approach, they invite readers on a journey of intellectual discovery, encouraging them to question established narratives and broaden their understanding of human history.

**"The Shaolin Temple Story"** (2023) is a nonfiction story by Shi Yongxin, the Abbot of the Shaolin Temple Monastery in China. Writings and interviews are translated into English and illustrated with archival and contemporary photographs and illustrations by a publisher-led team. The first-person narrative explores the temple's unique practices and beliefs,

including martial arts, Chán Buddhism, and traditional health and healing practices. In addition to archival pictures and documents, hundreds of new photos of the Shaolin Temple were shot exclusively for this 448-page book. The book provides historical and cultural information about an institution in Chinese history and culture. One of the critical aspects of creating the story was to be familiar with Chinese Chán (Zen) practice and the Chinese language.

These examples demonstrate how historical nonfiction storytelling can create engaging and informative narratives that bring the past to life. They use narrative techniques, such as character development, scene-setting, and plot structure, to make historical events and figures relatable and compelling to modern readers. Where possible, photographs, illustrations, and visual documentation are used.

### Journalistic Nonfiction Storytelling

Journalistic nonfiction storytelling can explore complex issues and engage readers on a deeper emotional level. They use narrative techniques, such as character development and storytelling structure, to bring information to life and connect with readers personally.

**"The Water Will Come"** by Jeff Goodell, published in 2017, explores rising sea levels' impact on cities and communities worldwide. Goodell uses narrative techniques to bring the science and politics of climate change to life, telling the stories of people already feeling the effects of rising seas.

**"A Life Too Short"** by Ronald Reng - published in 2011, this book tells the story of Robert Enke, a German goalkeeper who suffered from depression and took his own life in 2009. Reng uses his relationship with Enke to explore the psychology of depression and the pressures of professional soccer.

**"The Sober Truth: Debunking the Bad Science Behind 12-Step Programs and the Rehab Industry,"** by Lance Dodes and Zachary Dodes - published in 2014, this book examines the science and culture of addiction treatment in the United States. The authors use narrative techniques to tell the stories of people who have struggled with addiction and to challenge conventional wisdom about how addiction should be treated.

**"Blowout: Corrupted Democracy, rogue State Russia, and the Richest, Most Destructive Industry on Earth"** (2021), Rachel Maddow. "With her trademark dark humor, Maddow takes us on a switchback journey around the globe, revealing the greed and incompetence of Big Oil and Gas along the way and drawing a surprising conclusion about why the Russian government hacked the 2016 U.S. election. She deftly shows how Russia's rich reserves of crude have, paradoxically, stunted its growth, forcing Vladimir Putin to maintain his power by spreading Russia's rot into its rivals, its neighbors, the West's most important alliances, and the United States. She examines how the oil and gas industry has weakened democracies in developed and developing countries, fouled oceans and rivers, and propped up authoritarian thieves and killers."

### Examples of Biographic Nonfiction Storytelling

First published in June of 1947, **"The Diary of a Young Girl"** (Autobiography) by Anne Frank is a poignant and powerful memoir that chronicles the life of Anne Frank, a

Jewish girl living in hiding during the Holocaust. Set during World War II, the book is comprised of Anne's diary entries, written over two years while she and her family were concealed in a secret annex in Amsterdam.

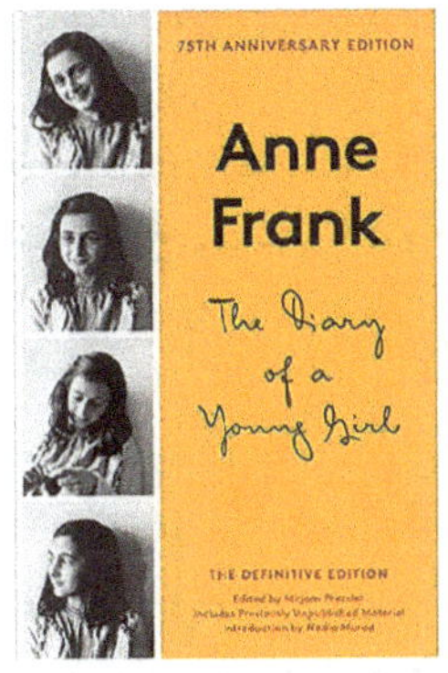

Through her diary, Anne opens a window into a young girl's daily struggles, hopes, and dreams grappling with adolescence and the extraordinary circumstances of her confinement. She vividly describes the challenges of living in close quarters with her family and the Van Pels family, along with the constant fear of discovery by the Nazis. Anne's writing captures the emotional turmoil, intellectual curiosity, and resilience that sustained her during this dark time.

Anne shares her aspirations, budding interest in writing, and reflections on the nature of humanity and the world around her. She finds solace in her diary, which she affectionately addresses as "Kitty," pouring her thoughts, fears, and dreams onto its pages. Through her words, Anne becomes a voice for millions of Holocaust victims, offering a personal and intimate account of the human spirit's endurance in the face of unimaginable adversity.

Tragically, Anne's diary ends abruptly, as her family is discovered and sent to concentration camps. Anne Frank herself perishes in the Holocaust, but her diary survives to bear witness to the horrors of that era and to inspire generations with its message of hope, courage, and the unwavering power of the human spirit. "The Diary of a Young

Girl" is a timeless testament to the strength and resilience of a young girl's indomitable spirit amidst the darkest times.

The writing style of *"The Diary of a Young Girl"* by Anne Frank can be described as intimate and introspective. Anne Frank's diary entries provide a firsthand account of her experiences and emotions while hiding from the Nazis in Amsterdam. The style is characterized by its honesty, vulnerability, and the personal connection it establishes with the reader.

Anne Frank's writing is marked by her ability to express her thoughts and feelings with remarkable clarity and depth. She often reflects on her inner struggles, hopes, dreams, and fears, providing insights into her personal growth and challenges during her confinement. The diary entries capture her youthful voice and the evolution of her perspectives as she navigates the complexities of adolescence amidst the backdrop of war.

This is an example of Anne Frank's writing style from her diary:

> *"Writing in a diary is a really strange experience for someone like me. Not only because I've never written anything before but also because it seems that later on, neither I nor anyone else will be interested in the musings of a thirteen-year-old schoolgirl. Oh well, it doesn't matter. I feel like writing."*

In this excerpt, Anne Frank acknowledges the uniqueness of her situation and her doubts about the significance of her diary. However, she continues to write, driven by her desire to express herself and find solace in putting her thoughts on paper. This above paragraph showcases her candid and introspective style, where she openly shares her thoughts about her writing and its potential impact.

The following examples demonstrate how biographic nonfiction storytelling can create compelling portraits of individuals and their lives. They use narrative techniques, such as dialogue, scene-setting, and emotional storytelling, to bring the personalities and experiences of their subjects to life and to engage readers on a deep and personal level.

**"Unbroken"** by Laura Hillenbrand - published in 2010, this book tells the story of Louis Zamperini, an Olympic athlete and World War II veteran who survived a plane crash 47 days adrift at sea two years in a Japanese POW camp. Hillenbrand uses narrative techniques to create a vivid and inspiring account of Zamperini's resilience and perseverance in the face of incredible adversity.

**"Alexander Hamilton"** by Ron Chernow - published in 2004, this book tells the story of the life and career of Alexander Hamilton, one of the Founding Fathers of the United States. Chernow uses narrative techniques to explore Hamilton's controversial legacy, his role in shaping the American government and finance, and his relationships and struggles.

**"Just Kids"** by Patti Smith - published in 2010, this book tells the story of the early years of Patti Smith's life and her relationship with the photographer Robert Mapplethorpe in New York City in the 1960s and 70s. Smith uses narrative techniques to evoke the atmosphere and culture of the time and to explore the creative and personal struggles of two young artists trying to make their way in the world.

## Memoirs

**"The Glass Castle"** (2009) by Jeannette Walls is a  memoir of resilience and redemption and a revelatory look into a family at once deeply dysfunctional and uniquely vibrant. When sober, Jeannette's brilliant and charismatic father captured his children's imagination, teaching them physics, geology, and how to embrace life fearlessly. But when he drank, he was dishonest and destructive. Her mother was a free spirit who abhorred the idea of domesticity and didn't want the responsibility of raising a family.

The Walls children learned to take care of themselves. They fed, clothed, and protected one another and eventually found their way to New York. Their parents followed them, choosing to be homeless even as their children prospered.

*"The Glass Castle"* (2009) by Jeannette Walls is a stirring memoir that merges stark honesty with vivid storytelling. Walls' nonfiction writing style is direct and unflinching yet imbued with a level of nostalgia that adds a layer of complexity to her account. Her voice carries a blend of candor, strength, and childlike wonder that permeates the narrative, even during its most distressing moments.

Walls unfolds her family's unconventional and chaotic life, with the narrative rooted in an almost paradoxical duality of hardship and love. Through her father, a man who oscillates between being an inspirational figure and a destructive force, she presents lessons of resilience, adventure, and a fearless embrace of life. Yet, his alcoholism introduces a dark undertone of dishonesty and volatility.

Her mother, an unconventional free spirit, serves as another focal point of the memoir. Through her, Walls brings to light the struggle between individuality and responsibility, adding depth to the overarching narrative of resilience and survival.

The transition of the Walls children from their tumultuous upbringing to prosperity in New York further underscores the theme of redemption. The stark contrast between their life and their parents' choice of homelessness adds a poignant layer to the narrative.

Throughout the memoir, Walls' style and voice remain consistent – she does not shy away from the stark realities of her upbringing. Yet, she also acknowledges the unconventional wisdom and life lessons it provided. In this way, Walls' memoir is not only a record of her family's dysfunctions and vibrancy but also a testament to her journey of accepting her past, navigating her present, and forging her future.

The memoir was made into a major motion picture in 2017, starring Brie Larson, Woody Harrelson, and Naomi Watts.

### Self-Help/Personal Development

**"The 7 Habits of Highly Effective People"** by Stephen R. Covey is a ground-breaking self-help book published in 1989. With over 25 million copies sold worldwide, it has become one of the most influential and widely recognized personal development books.

Covey presents a holistic approach to personal and professional effectiveness based on fundamental principles and habits that empower individuals to live with integrity, achieve their goals, and cultivate strong relationships. Covey introduces seven essential habits that, when practiced consistently, can lead to significant personal growth and effectiveness.

The book explores proactivity, beginning with the end in mind, prioritization, and the importance of effective communication and collaboration. Covey's teachings emphasize the development of a proactive mindset, aligning actions with core values, and fostering synergy through empathetic and collaborative interactions.

"*The 7 Habits of Highly Effective People*" resonates with readers worldwide, inspiring them to take charge of their lives, nurture positive habits, and build meaningful connections. Its enduring popularity and widespread impact highlight the universal relevance of Covey's principles and the enduring value they bring to personal and professional development.

"*The Writing Style of "The 7 Habits of Highly Effective People* " is primarily conversational and instructional rather than an active 2nd person style. The book predominantly employs a combination of active voice, descriptive storytelling, and practical guidance to engage readers and provide them with actionable insights.

"*The 7 Habits of Highly Effective People*" occasionally addresses the reader directly, encouraging them to reflect on their experiences and apply the principles. It only sometimes utilizes the second-person perspective throughout the entire text. Covey presents his ideas and concepts using a mix of personal anecdotes, case studies, and general examples to illustrate his points. This approach creates a sense of relatability and allows readers to connect with the material personally.

For example, Covey uses the story of the "Goose and the Golden Egg" to emphasize the importance of balancing production and production capability. He narrates how the farmer's greed in the story leads him to kill the goose, resulting in the loss of a consistent supply of golden eggs. This storytelling technique appeals to readers' imagination and helps them understand the underlying principle without directly addressing them as "you."

*"The 7 Habits of Highly Effective People"* writing style is a blend of narrative storytelling, instructional guidance, and relatable examples to engage readers and facilitate personal growth and effectiveness.

### Science

***"A Brief History of Time,"*** 1988 by Stephen Hawking, is a groundbreaking scientific work that explores the fundamental questions of the universe in a captivating and accessible manner. Hawking, a renowned physicist and cosmologist, presents complex scientific concepts in a way that makes them comprehensible to both scientific and non-scientific readers.

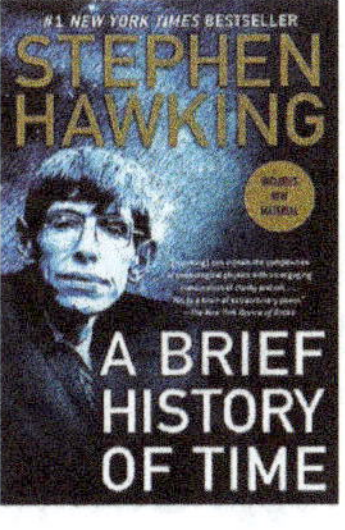


The book takes readers on a journey through the history of theoretical physics, from ancient cosmological beliefs to modern scientific advancements. Hawking discusses concepts such as the Big Bang theory, black holes, the nature of time, and the search for a unified approach to explain the universe's fundamental forces.

Hawking's writing style is characterized by clarity and simplicity, despite the complexity of the subject matter. He uses analogies, metaphors, and everyday examples to help readers grasp abstract concepts, making the book accessible to many audiences. The author's wit and occasional touches of humor add an engaging and relatable element to the narrative.

Throughout the book, Hawking intertwines scientific theories with philosophical ponderings, addressing profound questions about the origin and nature of the universe. He explores the implications of scientific discoveries and their potential impact on our understanding of existence.

"A Brief History of Time" provides a comprehensive overview of the critical concepts in cosmology and astrophysics and delves into the historical and cultural context in which these ideas emerged. It emphasizes the importance of scientific inquiry, critical thinking, and the ongoing pursuit of knowledge.

## Travel

**"Into the Wild"** by Jon Krakauer is not your typical travel book. But the main character is on a journey. Jon Krakauer constructs a clarifying prism through which he reassembles the disquieting facts of McCandless's short life. Krakauer searches for clues to the drives and desires that propelled McCandless.

McCandless gave $25,000 in savings to charity, abandoned his car and most possessions, burned all the cash in his wallet, and invented a new life. Not long after, he was dead. Into the Wild is the mesmerizing, heartbreaking tale of an enigmatic young man who goes missing in the wild and whose story captured the world's attention.

Immediately after graduating from college in 1991, McCandless roamed through the West and Southwest on a vision quest like those made by his heroes Jack London and John Muir. In the Mojave Desert, he abandoned his car, stripped it of its license plates, and burned all his cash. He assumed a new name, Alexander Supertramp. Leaving behind his desperate parents and sister, he vanished into the wild.

**"Eat, Pray, Love: One Woman's Search for Everything Across Italy, India, and Indonesia"** is a 2006 memoir by Elizabeth Gilbert that became a global bestseller and an iconic piece of travel literature. It details Gilbert's year-long journey worldwide after her difficult divorce and a crushing bout of depression. The book has three sections, each corresponding to a different country and aspect of Gilbert's self-discovery.

In the "Eat" portion of the book, Gilbert travels to Italy, indulging in the country's rich culinary culture and learning to appreciate the art of pleasure and the importance of nourishment not just for the body but also for the soul. The vivid descriptions of Italian food, culture, language, and people offer readers a vicarious journey through the gastronomic delights of Rome, Naples, and Sicily.

In "Pray," Gilbert journeys to an ashram in India, where she spends her days in meditation and spiritual practices, wrestling with her inner demons and seeking a connection with the divine. Here, readers get an inside look at the discipline and rigor of ashram life and a compelling exploration of Eastern spiritual traditions.

In "Love," Gilbert travels to Bali, Indonesia, where she seeks to find balance in her life and finds unexpected love. The lush tropical landscape of Bali forms a fitting backdrop to this exploration of love and companionship.

Throughout the book, Gilbert's warm and conversational writing style brings each location to life, vividly portraying each country's physical landscape and its cultural, spiritual, and culinary traditions. As a travel memoir, "Eat, Pray, Love" offers readers a profound and personal journey of self-discovery, healing, and transformation against the backdrop of three beautifully realized destinations. The book was made into a movie that did well at the box office.

### True Crime

**"I'll Be Gone in the Dark"** is a notable addition to the true crime genre, showcasing an exceptional blend of journalistic rigor and atmospheric narrative that is both engrossing and deeply unsettling. The book's title, "I'll Be Gone in the Dark," is a chilling echo of a taunt from the Golden State Killer to one of his victims, effectively setting the tone for what lies ahead.

Michelle McNamara's writing style is characterized by an intimate yet authoritative voice that pulls readers into the dark world of a serial rapist and killer who had eluded authorities for over four decades. McNamara's writing is not merely an account of cold facts and heinous crimes but an exploration of the human psyche—both Golden State Killer and her own. Her voice in the narrative is tenacious and compassionate, reflecting her unwavering commitment to seeking justice for the victims.

The book's narrative style unfolds with a cinematic quality, owing much to McNamara's background in screenwriting. The pacing is thoughtful, almost suspenseful, while the tone balances informative and unnerving. McNamara manages to create a sense of impending doom and uncertainty as she recreates scenes of the crimes, leading readers through the complex web of evidence, testimonies, and the haunting experiences of the victims.

In terms of structure, "*I'll Be Gone in the Dark*" presents a multi-layered narrative. It interweaves the story of the Golden State Killer with McNamara's personal life, her obsession with unsolved crimes, and her tireless pursuit to unmask the elusive criminal. The inclusion of personal anecdotes adds a poignant layer to the narrative, making it not only an actual crime investigation but also a study of the author's life, obsessions, and untimely death.

At the heart of McNamara's narrative is a profound empathy for the victims, highlighting violent crimes' devastating, lasting impacts. Her vivid descriptions of the crime scenes and their aftermath are harrowing, yet they serve an essential purpose: to bear witness to the victims' experiences and to bring their stories to the forefront. In doing so, McNamara's book is as much about giving voice to the silent victims as it is about uncovering the identity of the Golden State Killer.

"*I'll Be Gone in the Dark*" resonates with readers long after turning the final page. It stands as a testament to McNamara's dogged determination to unmask a notorious killer, and it remains a vital work in the field of authentic crime literature, a haunting examination of evil, obsession, and the relentless pursuit of justice.

## Philosophy

**"Meditations"** by Marcus Aurelius, 167 AD. "*Meditations*" is a series of personal reflections penned by Roman Emperor Marcus Aurelius. Often considered a cornerstone text in the philosophy of Stoicism, this work provides a deep look into Aurelius' thoughts on various topics, including virtue, rationality, self-improvement, and mortality. Composed in a time of significant military conflict and personal stress, the text encapsulates the Stoic tenet of finding peace and resilience amidst adversity.

Written in Greek, initially for personal guidance and self-improvement, the text is not a traditional philosophical treatise but a collection of thoughts and maxims. These notes were never intended for public consumption, which lends a sense of intimacy and authenticity to Aurelius' insights and musings.

The central theme of "*Meditations*" is the development of the Stoic philosophy of life. Aurelius emphasizes the rational understanding of the world, advising the reader to accept life's transience and the larger cosmic order. He often contemplates mortality, urging individuals to make the most of their lives in their short time.

"*Meditations*" also espouses the importance of virtues such as wisdom, justice, courage, and moderation. Aurelius provides advice on how to deal with different challenges and people, always reverting to the power of the mind and one's perception in shaping experiences.

Aurelius' reflections on the unity of the universe and the community of humankind are also significant aspects of the text, representing a spiritual interpretation of Stoic philosophy.

Despite being over 1800 years ago, the text remains relevant today, offering timeless wisdom and practical guidance on leading a good life. Its unpretentious and personal style makes it an approachable read, illuminating the mind of one of history's unique figures - a philosopher-king.

## Business/Economics:

**"The Lean Startup,"** written by entrepreneur and author Eric Ries in 2011, represents a compelling contribution to the literature on business and entrepreneurship. In this influential book, Ries presents his innovative approach to startup businesses, offering a new way to think about launching and managing ventures.

The writing style of *"The Lean Startup"* is approachable and engaging. Ries successfully breaks down complex concepts into digestible information, making the book accessible to individuals from various backgrounds, not just those in business. The language used is clear and direct, avoiding unnecessary jargon. However, when industry-specific terms are used, Ries defines and explains them, ensuring his readers are always aware of the situation.

Ries's voice in the narrative is authoritative yet supportive, reflecting his experiences as a serial entrepreneur. He maintains a conversational tone throughout, giving the feeling of a mentor sharing advice rather than a lecturer dictating terms. This creates a sense of camaraderie between the author and the reader, making the book feel personal and approachable.

The structure of *"The Lean Startup"* is methodical and iterative, mirroring the principles of the Lean Startup methodology. The book is divided into three parts: Vision, Steer, and Accelerate. Each part builds on the one before it, creating a roadmap for the reader.

In the "Vision" section, Ries outlines his philosophy and provides the foundational principles of the Lean Startup methodology. This sets the tone for the book and provides the context needed to understand the strategies and methods he describes later.

The "Steer" section is where Ries delves into how a Lean Startup operates. This is the book's heart, filled with case studies, examples, and detailed explanations. Here, the reader is introduced to key concepts such as the Build-Measure-Learn feedback loop and the Minimum Viable Product (MVP).

In the "Accelerate" section, Ries discusses how businesses can continue to innovate and adapt even as they grow larger. This part of the book provides insights on how to maintain the advantages of a startup - speed, agility, and customer focus - in a larger organization.

*"The Lean Startup"* effectively uses real-life examples and case studies to illustrate its points. These provide tangible samples readers can relate to, making the content more memorable and impactful. Using these narratives, Ries turns abstract concepts into concrete actions that readers can apply to their business ventures.

Overall, *"The Lean Startup"* is a powerful and practical guide for aspiring entrepreneurs or business leaders. Through his engaging writing style, authoritative voice, and structured narrative, Ries offers readers a novel approach to creating and managing successful startups. His ability to present complex business concepts in an easy-to-understand manner sets this book apart in the genre of business literature.

### Psychology and Psychotherapy

*"Man's Search for Meaning,"* 2006, by Viktor E. Frankl, is a profound piece of literature that explores Frankl's experiences as a prisoner in Nazi concentration camps during World War II and his post-war development of logotherapy, a form of existentialist psychotherapy. The book has become one of the most influential works 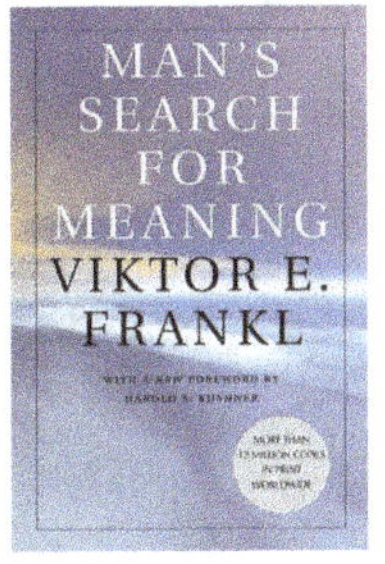
in psychology due to its unique blend of autobiographical narrative and psychological exploration.

Frankl's writing style is clear, direct, and philosophical. His language is imbued with the depth of his intellect, drawing on his vast knowledge of psychiatry and philosophy, yet remains accessible. He meticulously describes the minutiae of camp life and the emotional and psychological experiences of the prisoners, allowing readers to comprehend the situation's intensity.

The book is structured into two main parts, each serving a distinct purpose. The first part, "Experiences in a Concentration Camp," is a recollection of Frankl's time in the camps, serving as an autobiographical narrative that vividly illustrates the extreme conditions of human existence. This narrative lays the foundation for the book's second part, "Logotherapy in a Nutshell," where Frankl introduces his therapeutic approach.

Frankl's voice is imbued with compassion, wisdom, and resilience throughout the narrative. Despite the harsh realities he describes, his narrative is never devoid of hope. His voice is authoritative, reflective, and inherently human, adding depth to his experiences and the psychological theories he develops.

In presenting his theories, Frankl seamlessly integrates them within his narrative, making complex psychological concepts relatable and understandable. His theory of logotherapy, for example, posits that meaning in life is found through overcoming suffering, experiencing love, and creating a work or doing a deed, which is directly tied to his experiences in the concentration camps. His firsthand experiences bring a visceral authenticity to his theories and ideas, lending them a unique and profound weight.

Frankl's use of psychological terms is sparing and measured. He presents complex psychological theories in layperson's terms, ensuring the book's accessibility to a broad audience. When he does use specific psychological terms, he carefully explains them, providing that readers without a background in psychology can understand and appreciate his insights.

In *"Man's Search for Meaning,"* Frankl masterfully interweaves narrative, psychological insight, and philosophical pondering. His straightforward writing style, compassionate and wise voice, and the careful structure of his narrative create an enduring work that resonates deeply with readers, encouraging them to contemplate the nature of suffering, the quest for meaning, and the resilience of the human spirit.

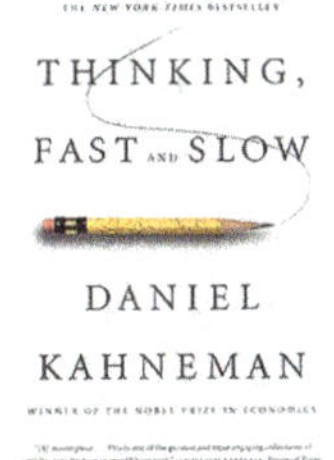

***"Thinking, Fast and Slow,"*** 2013, is a seminal work by psychologist and Nobel laureate Daniel Kahneman. In it, Kahneman delves into the two systems of thought that govern our minds: System 1, which is fast and intuitive, and System 2, which is slow and deliberate. The book, lauded for its in-depth examination of decision-making and behavioral economics, is as much a psychology study as it is a testament to Kahneman's extensive career.

The writing style of *"Thinking, Fast and Slow"* is scholarly yet accessible, a nod to Kahneman's academic background and commitment to bringing psychological insights to a broad audience. Despite the complexity of the subject matter, Kahneman employs a clear, concise, and jargon-free style that brings readers into the complex workings of the mind. His writing is characterized by deep insight and curiosity, making the book fascinating, even for those not in psychology.

Kahneman's voice throughout the book is measured, reflective, and candid. He doesn't shy away from addressing his ideas' limitations and potential criticisms, an attribute that adds credibility to his work. His honesty, particularly when discussing his decision-making errors and cognitive biases, injects a degree of relatability and humor into the narrative.

The structure of "*Thinking, Fast and Slow*" is arranged into five distinct parts, each addressing a different aspect of cognitive function and decision-making. The first part introduces the two systems of thought, setting the foundation for the ideas developed in the subsequent sections. The second and third parts delve into heuristics and biases, exploring how these impact our thinking and decision-making processes. The fourth part discusses prospect theory, a model of decision-making that Kahneman developed with Amos Tversky. Finally, the fifth part explores the concept of two selves—the experiencing self and the remembering self—and how they affect our perception of happiness.

One of the book's unique features is the use of thought experiments to illustrate complex psychological phenomena. These experiments invite readers to engage actively with the text and effectively highlight the book's key concepts. They serve to make abstract psychological theories tangible and applicable to everyday life.

Overall, "*Thinking, Fast and Slow*" is an influential book that shines a light on our cognitive processes, decision-making, and biases. Kahneman's accessible writing style, thoughtful voice, and well-structured narrative make the complexities of psychology understandable and relevant to a broad audience, from students and academics to curious lay readers.

## Practical or Instructional Nonfiction

**"Win Every Argument"** by Mehdi Hasan (2023) comes under self-help or practical nonfiction. The book provides practical advice and strategies for improving one's argumentative skills. While the book uses real-world examples to illustrate its points, it primarily focuses on providing helpful tips and strategies rather than an in-depth analysis of the theory or history of argumentation. It is a personal strategy based on the author's experience and point of view. "*Win Every Argument*" is a nonfiction book that aims to help readers improve their argumentative skills.

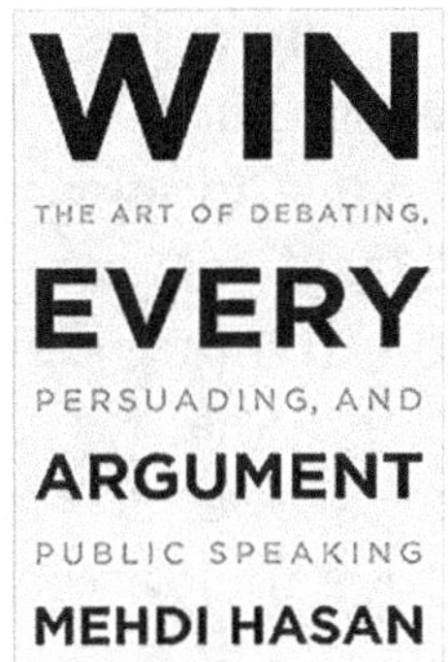


Hasan's writing style is clear and concise, making the book easy to read and understand. He writes in a first-person, friendly manner. He uses simple language and avoids technical jargon, making the book accessible to a broad audience. The content is well organized. "*Win Every Argument*" is divided into clear sections, each focusing on a different aspect of argumentation. Hasan uses subheadings, bullet points, and summaries to help readers navigate the content and understand the main points. He includes practical advice. The book provides helpful tips and strategies for effective argumentation, such as understanding your opponent's perspective, avoiding logical fallacies, and using persuasive language. Hasan uses real-world examples to illustrate his points, making the advice more relatable and applicable. The story focuses primarily on argumentation in a political context. However, the concepts carry over to other areas. It may be helpful for readers looking to improve their argumentation skills in different contexts, such as business or personal relationships.

The book provides valuable tips and strategies and briefly looks deeper into the underlying theories or principles of argumentation. As the text indicates, readers looking for a more theoretical or academic approach may want additional research. "*Win Every Argument*" by Mehdi Hasan is a well-written and practical guide to argumentation that provides valuable tips and strategies for improving argumentative skills. While it may be limited in theoretical scope, it is a worthwhile read for anyone looking to improve their ability to make persuasive arguments in a political context and issues more mundane.

Please note that these are a few examples, and numerous other nonfiction books are available in each genre category. Also, nonfiction includes a vast range of genres and topics. These examples demonstrate how nonfiction storytelling can explore complex and essential issues, connect with audiences emotionally, and provide insights and understanding that would be difficult to convey through other media. Nonfiction writing covers an immense area of subjects, topics, and genres. Find nonfiction books written in the same genre you are interested in. Anyone wanting to write nonfiction should read nonfiction.

There are many styles and approaches to telling nonfiction stories. Decide which writing styles engage you most, then decide on your path.

# CHAPTER 3

## Writing Nonfiction Stories

Writing a nonfiction story can be complex and challenging, but with the right approach, it can also be a rewarding and fulfilling experience. Developing a narrative structure begins with writing clear and concise prose and using descriptive language and sensory details.

### Developing a Narrative Structure

Start with an idea or concept. Begin by identifying a subject or topic you are passionate about and interested in exploring. This will motivate and inspire you to develop a compelling narrative structure. Documentary projects usually begin with a concept and treatment. A "concept" enlarges on an idea detailing how it may be expanded, with a beginning, middle, and end. This approach can be applied to a book project as well. The treatment details in a narrative outline how the subject will be approached.

Once you have a clear idea of your nonfiction story, outline the main points and ideas you want to cover. This will help you organize your thoughts and ensure your narrative flows smoothly.

Identify a protagonist. Every good story, fiction or nonfiction, needs a protagonist, central character, or theme the reader can identify. This could be an actual person, place, or event you are exploring.

Build a narrative arc: A good nonfiction story needs a beginning, middle, and end. The narrative arc should be structured to build tension, create conflict, and resolve the story.

## Write Clear and Concise Prose

Know your audience. Understanding your target audience is vital to writing clear and concise prose. Use language and terminology they will understand and avoid jargon or technical terms that might confuse or alienate your readers. Keep it simple. Avoid using overly complicated sentences or complex language. Write clearly and straightforwardly in a way that is easy to understand. Use active voice. Active voice is more engaging and accessible to read than passive voice. Use strong verbs and action-oriented language to keep your readers engaged.

## Use Descriptive Language and Sensory Details

Paint a picture: Use descriptive language to create vivid and engaging descriptions of people, places, and events. Use sensory details such as sight, sound, smell, and touch to bring your story to life. Show rather than tell. Instead of telling your readers what is happening, show them through vivid and engaging descriptions. This will help to immerse your readers in the story and create a more immersive and engaging experience. Use metaphors and similes: Metaphors and similes can be powerful tools for creating descriptive language and engaging readers' imaginations. Use them sparingly but effectively to add depth and richness to your prose.

### Edit ruthlessly

Once you have written a first draft of your nonfiction story, go back and edit it ruthlessly. Cut out unnecessary words and phrases and tighten up your prose to make it as concise and impactful as possible. Use a grammar and spelling checker like Grammarly Pro to check your text. There are other applications available if you don't like Grammarly.

### Research

Based on real-world events and experiences, nonfiction stories require thorough research. This may include conducting interviews, gathering data and information, and verifying sources to ensure accuracy and credibility. The critical elements of a nonfiction story should work together to create a compelling and informative narrative that engages and enlightens the reader. Nonfiction can be written in a narrative, descriptive, or expository style.

Research is a crucial step in nonfiction storytelling, and it involves finding and evaluating sources, conducting interviews, and organizing research. Here are some tips on conducting effective research for a nonfiction story.

### Finding and Evaluating Sources

Start by identifying the sources you need for your story: books, articles, archives, government records, or online sources. Use a variety of sources to ensure a well-rounded perspective. Evaluate sources for accuracy, credibility, and relevance. Look for reputable sources with a track record of producing high-quality information.

### Conducting Interviews

Identify potential interview sources, such as experts, witnesses, or individuals with first-hand experience related to your story[1]. Plan your questions to ensure you cover all your story's relevant aspects. Be respectful and professional during the interview and take notes or record the conversation to ensure accuracy.

## Organizing Research

Once you have gathered all your research material, create a system for organizing it. This could be a physical system, such as filing folders, or a digital system, such as a spreadsheet or note-taking app. Ensure you clearly understand the material you have collected and categorize it according to relevance to your story.

### Additional Tips for Effective Research

- Be open-minded and flexible when conducting research. You may uncover information that challenges your initial assumptions or changes the direction of your story.
- Use a variety of sources to ensure a balanced perspective. Don't rely on a single authority or a particular viewpoint.
- Keep track of your sources and citations. This will ensure that you can easily reference them later and avoid plagiarism.
- Be patient and persistent. Research can be time-consuming, but it is essential for creating a well-researched and informative nonfiction story.
- Critical Evaluation: Not all sources are created equal. Evaluate the credibility of the sources you are using. Check their authorship, date of publication, and any potential biases. This is particularly important when using online resources.

---

1 Actuality Interviewing and Listening, 2017,2023

- Comprehensive Exploration: Look beyond the most obvious sources. For instance, if you're researching a historical event, rely on something other than textbooks or popular accounts - delve into primary source materials like letters, diaries, and newspaper articles from the time.
- Organization: Keep your research materials organized. Creating a system for noting where you found certain pieces of information is helpful.
- Fact-Checking: Cross-verify the facts from multiple sources. Misinformation spreads easily. Checking facts from various reliable sources can help ensure accuracy.
- Notes: Make detailed notes as you go along, including a summary of the information, quotes, and your thoughts or ideas that might arise from reading. These will be invaluable when you start writing.
- Time Management: Set aside specific blocks of time for research. It can be easy to lose track of time when you're deep into researching, so setting limits can help keep you focused and efficient.
- Communication: If you're using interviews as part of your research, remember that effective communication is critical. Ask straightforward, open-ended questions that encourage detailed responses.

Online resources like Google can be a treasure trove of information for researching nonfiction writing, but they also present unique challenges. Here are some tips to effectively utilize these resources:

- Use Advanced Search Techniques: Get familiar with Google's advanced search functions. For instance, using quotation marks around a phrase will yield results where those words appear together in that order. You can also use operators like AND, OR, and NOT to refine your search.

- Scholarly Databases: Google Scholar can be a valuable tool for accessing academic papers, articles, books, theses, and conference papers. Many of these resources have undergone peer review, adding to their credibility.

- Website Domain: Look at the website domain -.edu, .gov, and .org sites tend to be more reliable, although this is only sometimes the case. Be extra vigilant when using commercial (.com) sites.

- Author Credibility: Check the author's credentials and background to gauge their expertise.

- Cross-Verification: Verify information from multiple credible sources to ensure accuracy.

- Date of Publication: Be mindful of the date of the information. Recent sources are often more reliable, especially in science, medicine, technology, and current events.

- Bias Detection: Be aware of potential biases in the sources. Every source has a perspective; understanding this can help critically analyze the information.

- Citation: When you find valuable and credible information, cite it properly. Many online articles will have a "how to cite this" tool.

- Utilize Libraries Online: Many libraries offer online resources, including access to databases that are only sometimes available to the public.

- Save Information: Save the information you find by downloading it or using a tool like Google Drive or OneNote. Include the source URL, especially if it's a webpage that might change.

While Google and the internet can provide much valuable information, they shouldn't be the only tools you use for research. Be sure to combine them with other resources like books, scholarly articles, interviews, and primary sources to give your research depth and variety.

Research is a vital part of nonfiction writing. Ensure that your research is thorough, accurate, and supports your writing.

## Use Descriptive Language and Sensory Details

Paint a picture: Use descriptive language to create vivid and engaging descriptions of people, places, and events. Use sensory details such as sight, sound, smell, and touch to bring your story to life. Show rather than tell. Instead of telling your readers what is happening, show them through vivid and engaging descriptions. This will help to immerse your readers in the story and create a more immersive and engaging experience. Use metaphors and similes: Metaphors and similes can be powerful tools for creating descriptive language and engaging readers' imaginations. Use them sparingly but effectively to add depth and richness to your prose.

Be selective: While descriptive language and sensory details are essential, it's also important to be selective in how and when you use them. Use them to highlight key moments or to add depth and richness to your prose but use them sparingly to the point where they become distracting or overwhelming.

## Writing Guidelines

Identify the strengths and limitations of each medium. Different media have different strengths and limitations in conveying information and engaging audiences. The writer should identify the strengths and limitations of each medium and adjust accordingly.

Adapt the story for each medium. The writer should adapt the story to suit the strengths and limitations of each medium. For example, a print story may require more descriptive language, while a video story may require more visual elements.

Use appropriate visuals and graphics. Visuals and graphics can enhance the impact of a nonfiction story. The writer should select visuals and pictures for each medium to support the narrative and add to the story's overall impact.

The length of the story can vary depending on the medium. Adjust the length as needed to suit the medium and the audience. For example, a video story may need to be shorter than a print story. It is not an excellent policy to stretch an account to make it fill a certain amount of time or pages.

The pacing of a nonfiction story can affect its impact across different media. Consider the story's pacing and adjust it to suit the medium. For example, a video story may require a faster pace than a print story. Presenting a nonfiction story across different media requires careful consideration of the strengths and limitations of each medium and the ability to adapt the story to suit each medium. The writer should use appropriate visuals and graphics and adjust the length and pacing of the story.

Pay attention to sound and music. Sound and music can enhance the impact of a nonfiction story in audio and video media. The presenter should select sound and music that support the narrative and add to the story's overall impact.

Presenting a nonfiction story across different media involves adapting the story to suit the strengths and limitations of each medium. Nonfiction stories can be told in various media, including print, audio, and video. For example, video stories may require more visual elements, while audio stories may require more descriptive language. Music and effects can help tell the story or, if used indiscriminately, distract from the narrative.

## Editing and Revising

Editing and revising are crucial steps in the nonfiction storytelling process, as they help refine and improve the quality of your story. One valuable aspect of the editing and revising process is obtaining peer review and feedback. The importance of peer review and input in nonfiction storytelling should be considered.

Peer review allows you to receive feedback from individuals who bring a fresh perspective to your work. They can offer insights, suggestions, and constructive criticism that you may need to look into due to your familiarity with the material. Their input can help identify areas for improvement and offer new ideas to enhance your nonfiction story.

Peers can provide an objective assessment of your work. They can assess whether your nonfiction story achieves its intended goals, effectively communicates its message, and resonates with the target audience. Peer reviewers can identify inconsistencies, gaps in information, or areas where further clarification is needed.

Peer review gathers feedback from individuals with diverse backgrounds, experiences, and perspectives. This diversity ensures a broader range of feedback, which can enrich your nonfiction story and help you consider multiple angles or alternative viewpoints. It helps ensure your account appeals to a wider audience and addresses potential concerns or biases.

Peer review is a quality control mechanism for your nonfiction story. Through their feedback, peers can highlight areas requiring further research, fact-checking, or verification. They can also point out grammatical, structural, or stylistic issues that may hinder the readability and impact of your story. Their insights can help you enhance the overall quality of your work.

Peer feedback can provide proof and encouragement during the editing and revising. This includes validation and encouragement. Constructive criticism can highlight the strengths of your nonfiction story and areas where you excel. Positive feedback can motivate you to continue refining your work, knowing it resonates with others.

## *Effective Peer Review and Feedback*

Choose your peers wisely. Seek feedback from knowledgeable individuals or experts in the subject matter and those who can provide a fresh perspective. Provide clear guidelines: Communicate what aspects of your nonfiction story you would like feedback on. Specify if you want structure, clarity, style, or specific content feedback.

Be open-minded and receptive—approach peer review with an open mind and a willingness to accept constructive criticism. Be receptive to different viewpoints and suggestions, even if they challenge your initial ideas. Seek a balance of perspectives. Gather feedback from diverse peers to ensure a well-rounded evaluation. Consider seeking input from individuals with different backgrounds, experiences, and expertise.

Prioritize actionable feedback. Focus on feedback with specific suggestions or actionable insights to improve your nonfiction story. It's helpful to receive feedback that goes beyond general opinions and offers concrete ways to enhance your work. By actively engaging in peer review and feedback, you can refine and strengthen your nonfiction story, making it more impactful, engaging, and informative for your readers.

Polishing the final draft of a nonfiction story is a crucial step in the editing and revising process. It involves fine-tuning the details, ensuring clarity, enhancing the overall readability, and making the story as compelling and engaging as possible. Here are some key aspects to consider when polishing the final draft of your nonfiction story. While these aspects refer to finishing a book or print project, they generally apply to all media, including video and audio.

Strive for clarity and coherence. Review your nonfiction story for clarity and coherence at both the macro and micro levels. Ensure the overall structure flows smoothly, with logical transitions between sections or chapters. At the sentence and paragraph level, pay attention to clarity and eliminate any ambiguity or confusion.

Refine your language and writing style to make the nonfiction story more engaging and accessible to your readers. Strive for a balance between formal and conversational tone, depending on the subject matter and intended audience. Use precise and descriptive language. Consider the pacing and rhythm of your sentences to create a smooth reading experience.

Pay close attention to grammar, punctuation, and spelling. Correct grammatical errors and eliminate typos. Ensure consistent punctuation throughout the story. Consider using proofreading tools or seeking assistance from a professional editor to catch any overlooked mistakes.

Fact-checking and accuracy are essential. Double-check all the information presented in your story. Verify facts, statistics, and references to ensure their reliability. Cross-reference your sources and make sure the story reflects accurate and up-to-date information. This step is crucial to maintain credibility and avoid potential inaccuracies.

Trim unnecessary content. Review the manuscript to identify and remove excessive or repetitive content. Streamline your narrative to focus on the essential elements and eliminate any tangents or digressions that do not contribute to the overall message or flow of the story.

Look for opportunities to enhance your storytelling techniques. Consider using vivid descriptions, anecdotes, and narrative devices to captivate your readers and bring your story to life. Use storytelling elements such as plot development, character arcs, and conflict resolution to engage your audience.

Seek external feedback: Consider seeking input from beta readers, editors, or trusted individuals who can provide an objective perspective on your final draft. External feedback can help you identify unsupported subjective spots, uncover areas that may need further improvement, and provide valuable insights for enhancing the overall impact of your nonfiction story.

Read aloud and revise: Take the time to read your final draft aloud. This allows you to catch awkward phrasing, pacing issues, or unclear passages. Revise and refine these sections accordingly to ensure a smooth reading experience.

Look for formatting and presentation issues. Pay attention to the visual representation of your nonfiction story. Ensure consistent design, font styles, and headings throughout the document. Use appropriate subheadings, bullet points, and formatting techniques to improve readability and help readers navigate the content easily.

Final proofreading is necessary. Conduct a final proofread of your polished draft before publishing or sharing it with others. Pay attention to any last-minute errors or inconsistencies that may have been missed during editing.

This final check ensures that your nonfiction story is as polished and error-free as possible. By carefully polishing the final draft, you can refine your nonfiction story to its fullest potential, ensuring it is engaging, informative, and compelling for your readers.

Editing and revising nonfiction stories in various media involves several considerations, depending on the medium used.

### Identify the Purpose and Audience

The purpose and intended audience of the nonfiction story will determine the tone, style, and level of detail needed. This information should guide the editing and revision process.

### Review for accuracy

Nonfiction stories should be based on verifiable facts and sources. Carefully review the writing to ensure all information presented is accurate and supported by evidence. If necessary, consult with experts on the subject to verify the information.

### Check for Consistency

Review the story for consistency in facts, tone, style, and voice. Inconsistencies can distract readers and detract from the story's overall impact.

### Check Pacing

The pacing of a nonfiction story is essential to keep the reader engaged. The editor reviews the story for pacing, ensuring it is consistent.

## Remove Extraneous Information

Stories can become weighed down by irrelevant information that does not contribute to the narrative. Editing should remove any unnecessary information that detracts from the story. Determine if the data adds a significant fact to the description or subject.

## Enhance Readability

Review the story for readability, ensuring it is easy to understand and follow. This may involve breaking up long paragraphs or simplifying complex ideas.

Pay attention to the structure. The structure of a story can affect its impact. Review the story for design, ensuring a clear beginning, middle, and end.

### Understand the Medium That You Are Editing

Overall, editing and revising nonfiction stories requires attention to detail, consideration of the intended audience, and a willingness to make revisions that enhance the story's impact. If you can afford it, hire an editor to read your manuscript and make recommendations. Another alternative is to have someone whose opinion you trust read the draft. Expect them to be critically constructive in their review. Keep the feedback in mind and read your manuscript, making any changes that come to mind. Before the manuscript is finished, you will still need an editor to review it for editorial considerations. It is challenging to edit your manuscript by yourself. This is not necessarily because you are self-indulgent. Because you are familiar with the story, you may gloss over sentences and paragraphs without reading every word. If you must edit, use an app like Grammarly Premium and take your time. Reading your manuscript aloud is an excellent way to find mistakes and awkward phrasing. Finally, review your manuscript for style consistency and redundancy, especially if you have been working on the story for an extended period.

## SEO Writing for Internet Publications

SEO writing stands for "Search Engine Optimization."It is a way of creating content for websites or online platforms designed to attract more visitors through search engines like Google, Bing, or Yahoo. The main goal of SEO writing is to improve visibility in search results, making it easier for people to find the content when they search for related topics.

In simpler terms, SEO writing is about crafting content that makes it more likely to appear on the first page of search engine results when someone searches for a particular keyword or topic. By appearing higher in the search results, a website has a better chance of getting more organic traffic, leading to more readers, customers, or followers.

**Keyword Research:** Identifying the words or phrases (keywords) that people commonly use when searching for information about the topic you want to write about. For instance, if you're writing a blog about healthy recipes, you might find that "easy healthy dinner recipes" is a popular keyword. You would then incorporate that keyword strategically into your content. Keywords also play a part in picking a title for your work.

The following is a list of SEO keywords used in the "Forward" of this book, page "X." The Forward is the basis for our description online. It will help search engines find the book. There may be a bit of over-kill here, but it covers two pages.

- Nonfiction writing
- Journey
- Exploration
- Creativity
- Self-expression
- Professional writer
- Aspiring
- Communication skills
- Guide
- Compelling narratives
- Memoirs
- Biographies
- Essays
- Journalism
- Genres
- Styles
- Art of storytelling
- Real-life events
- Captivating ideas
- Empower
- Compass
- Tools
- Knowledge
- Inspiration
- Research process
- Interviews
- Fact-checking
- Authentic voice
- Engaging readers
- Ordinary moments
- Extraordinary tales
- Ethical responsibilities
- Empathy
- Fairness
- Respect
- Enriching journey
- Skillfully
- Gather information
- Transform
- Truth
- Accuracy
- Distinct perspective
- Forge connections
- Power of storytelling
- Inspire
- Educate
- Ignite change
- Writing exercises
- Feedback
- Seasoned nonfiction writers
- Craft
- Experiment
- Take risks
- Joy of discovery
- Refine
- Awe-inspiring
- Literary world
- Invigorating
- Grasp your pen
- Transformative adventure
- Unearth hidden stories
- Unique perspective
- Journey of a lifetime.

## Title Optimization

Craft catchy and relevant titles that include your target keywords. For example, using the keyword "best budget smartphones" in the title of a technology article can make it more appealing to search engines and potential readers.

**Quality Content:** Write informative, engaging, and valuable content that addresses the needs of your target audience. Search engines prioritize content that provides real value to users, so well-written and helpful articles rank higher.

**Meta Tags:** Including relevant meta tags like meta descriptions and meta titles, which are summaries that appear in search results. These tags should contain keywords and a compelling call to action to attract clicks.

**Link Building:** Obtaining links from other reputable websites to your content, as search engines consider backlinks a sign of authority and relevance.

**User-Friendly Formatting:** Using short paragraphs, bullet points, headings, and subheadings to make your content easy to read and understand, both for readers and search engines.

The aim of SEO writing is not only to impress search engines but to provide value to your audience. If your content satisfies the needs of your readers, it's likely to perform well in search results and bring in more traffic over time.

# Chapter 4

# Nonfiction Formats

Presenting a nonfiction story in print involves considerations of writing for different formats, formatting the layout effectively, and selecting compelling visuals and graphics. Let's explore each of these areas in more detail.

## Writing for Specific Formats

When presenting a nonfiction story in print, it's essential to adapt your writing style and approach to suit different formats.

### Nonfiction Books

In a full-length nonfiction book, you have the space to delve deeply into a topic, provide ample background information, elaborate on details, and develop complex ideas. The narrative may take on a more formal, structured tone, and you can explore different narrative techniques, such as linear or non-linear storytelling or alternating perspectives.

There are many different categories of books. However, whatever the subject, develop a clear structure for each chapter, ensuring a logical flow of ideas and seamless transitions. Use supporting evidence, anecdotes, and examples to strengthen your arguments or narratives.

Incorporate subheadings, bullet points, and other formatting elements to enhance readability. Each chapter in a nonfiction book adds to the information and storyline for the entire book. Nonfiction stories have a beginning, middle, and end, much like an essay. The chapters fit together to tell a complete story. Suppose you are writing a book about "Climate Change." Your early chapters might discuss the types of change and where they are happening. Middle chapters, the reasons for these changes. Final chapters, possible remedies, and conclusions.

## Layout and Design

The layout of a nonfiction story in print significantly impacts the reader's experience. The design is composed of the following areas.

The right **typography** is essential for the book. Choose appropriate fonts for the text, headings, and subheadings that match the tone and style of your nonfiction story. Ensure legibility by using proper font size and line spacing. Choose a font that matches the tone and seriousness of the topic.

**Paragraph and Sentence Structure** is critical. Break up large blocks of text into shorter sections to enhance readability. Utilize varied sentence lengths and structures to maintain a dynamic and engaging flow.

**Headings and Subheadings** help the reader understand the meaning of the paragraph. Clearly label sections and subsections with informative and descriptive headings and subheadings. This aids readers in navigating through the content and finding relevant information quickly.

**Visual Hierarchy** should be consistent. Use formatting techniques such as bolding, italics, and bullet points to highlight key points, important information, or quotes. This helps to create a visual hierarchy and draws attention to critical elements. Consult a style guide for standard hierarchy usage.

**Choose Compelling Visuals and Graphics**. Visual elements can significantly enhance the presentation of a nonfiction story in print. Consider these areas when selecting visuals and graphics.

**Photographs, images, and illustrations** help to tell the story. Choose high-quality, relevant pictures and graphics that support and enrich your narrative. Ensure proper attribution and permissions for any copyrighted material. Captions can provide additional context or information.

**Use infographics, charts, and graphs** to visually represent data, statistics, or complex information. These visuals can make the content more accessible and engaging for readers.

**Consider using illustrations or maps** to visually depict locations, historical events, or concepts discussed in your nonfiction story. These visuals can provide clarity and help readers better understand the subject matter.

**Include informative captions or labels for visuals and graphics** to provide context, explanations, or additional details that complement the written content.

## Writing Style

Presenting a nonfiction story in print involves carefully adapting your writing style to different formats, creating an appealing layout, and incorporating compelling visuals and graphics. Considering these elements, you can effectively engage your readers and enhance their understanding and enjoyment of your nonfiction story.

## Book Cover

It has been said that "we should not judge a book by its cover." This remains true. But from a marketing standpoint, the cover of your book is the first thing most people see before they know anything about the contents of the book. The book cover of your book must not be an afterthought. The book cover of your book should help sell the book. You can begin considering ideas for the cover while writing the book. Consult with a book cover designer.

## Magazine Articles

In contrast to a book, a magazine article is usually shorter, more targeted, and immediately engaging. Your writing style needs to be more concise. Magazine articles typically have limited space and require concise, engaging writing. Capture the reader's attention with a compelling introduction, maintain a clear and focused narrative, and use subheadings to organize your content effectively. Craft your writing to align with the tone and style of the specific magazine you are targeting. Obtain a copy of the magazine for which you would like to write. Read the articles to gain insight into the publication's style.

## Academic Papers

An academic paper requires a formal, and objective tone. You should use precise language and provide clear evidence to support your arguments. It's also essential to follow the specific citation style for your field. The narrative flow might be less important here than in other formats, with a focus instead on clear, logical argumentation.

## Blog Posts

A blog post is usually more casual and conversational. The writing might be more personal, with anecdotes or experiences often forming part of the narrative. In this format, it's also common to break up text with subheadings, bullet points, images, or infographics to make it more web-friendly. Write posts with Search Engine Optimization (SEO) priorities in mind. There are methods you can use to determine keywords or phrases.

Here are several enhanced techniques for creating SEO-friendly blog articles:

**Keyword Research:** The first step is identifying commonly searched words or phrases relevant to your article's topic. These are known as keywords. For instance, if your blog post is about air travel, "best airlines" could be a keyword. Integrate these keywords organically within your content to optimize searchability.

**Title Optimization:** Craft engaging and pertinent titles that incorporate your target keywords. For example, if you're writing a tech piece on electric cars, a title like "Exploring the Best Mileage Electric Cars" can be more appealing to search engines and potential readers.

**Valuable Content:** Develop informative, engaging content that addresses your target audience's needs. Search engines prioritize content offering genuine value to users; thus, well-structured and insightful articles tend to secure higher rankings.

**Meta Tags:** Utilize appropriate meta tags such as meta descriptions and meta titles. These concise summaries, visible in search results, should incorporate keywords to attract more clicks.

**Backlinks:** Aim to acquire links from other reputable websites directed to your content. Search engines perceive these backlinks as indications of your content's relevance and authority.

**Readable Format:** Deploying shorter paragraphs, bullet points, headings, and subheadings can enhance the readability of your blog post for both readers and search engines.

By employing these SEO writing techniques, your goal should be to cater to search engines and your audience. Producing high-quality content that provides the information your audience seeks can enhance search engine performance, attract more readers, and increase website traffic.

### Podcast Scripts

If your nonfiction story is presented as a podcast, you must write in a conversational tone, as if speaking directly to the listener. The language should be engaging and straightforward, and you can use narrative techniques such as suspense, surprise, or emotion to keep the listener's interest.

While the core information remains the same in all these formats, how you present it can change significantly. Understanding the norms and expectations of each format will help you adapt your writing style and approach effectively, ensuring that your nonfiction story resonates with its intended audience.

## Nonfiction writing for animation or slide presentations.

Creating an animated nonfiction story involves a unique blend of storytelling, visual design, and animation techniques. Here are the steps involved in writing and creating an animated nonfiction story.

### Define Your Objectives and Audience

Determine the purpose of your animated nonfiction story. Clarify the main message or takeaway you want to convey. Identify your target audience and tailor your storytelling approach to engage and educate them effectively.

### Research and Gather Information

Conduct thorough research on your chosen nonfiction topic. Collect reliable and relevant information from credible sources such as books, articles, documentaries, and interviews. Organize and synthesize the information to form the basis of your story.

### Develop the Narrative Structure

Outline the key points, themes, and structure of your story. Determine the main story arc and how you will present the information logically and engagingly. Decide on your story's beginning, middle, and end, ensuring a clear and cohesive narrative flow.

## Write the Script

Craft a script that translates the nonfiction content into a compelling, concise narrative suitable for animation. Write dialogue, voiceover narration, and on-screen text effectively conveying the information. Remember the visual elements accompanying the script and how they will enhance the storytelling.

## Create Storyboards

Visualize the key scenes and sequences of your animated nonfiction story through storyboards. Sketch each scene's visual composition, camera angles, character poses, and transitions. Storyboards serve as a blueprint for the animation process and help maintain optical coherence.

## Design the Visual Style

Determine the visual style and aesthetic for your animated nonfiction story. Consider the tone, mood, and subject matter of the story. Develop character designs, background art, color schemes, and other visual elements to bring the story to life. Ensure the visual style aligns with the intended audience and the story's objectives.

### Creating Animatics

Animatics are preliminary movie versions produced by shooting storyboard sections and adding a soundtrack. Produce animatics and rough animated sequences that combine the storyboards with the recorded dialogue or narration. Before committing to total production, animatics help you visualize the animation's timing, pacing, and overall flow. Make any necessary adjustments to the animatics to ensure the desired impact.

## Animation Production

Begin the animation production process, which involves creating individual frames or sequences based on the storyboards and animatics. This typically includes character animation, background artwork, visual effects, and any necessary compositing. Utilize appropriate software and tools for animation production, ensuring high-quality visuals and smooth movements.

## Sound Design and Music

Develop or select suitable sound effects and background music complementing the animated nonfiction story. Enhance the storytelling through audio elements that convey emotions, create ambiance, and highlight important moments. Ensure proper audio mixing and synchronization with the animation.

## Editing and Finalization

Review and edit the animated nonfiction story to ensure coherence, clarity, and quality. Make any necessary adjustments to the pacing, timing, or visuals. Seek feedback from trusted individuals or focus groups. Once satisfied, finalize the animation, and export it in the appropriate format for distribution across various platforms.

Throughout the process, balance entertainment and education, effectively conveying the nonfiction content while engaging the audience visually and emotionally. Collaboration with animators, designers, sound engineers, and other professionals is crucial to successfully bringing your animated nonfiction story to life.

## Slide Presentations

Creating a nonfiction slide presentation follows the same process as other visual presentations. Like an animated project, a script should be written for the story—a story with a beginning, middle, and end. Individual slides should be designed to be cut together to create continuity. A multicolumn script is ideal for previsualizing your presentation. The format is the same as the multicolumn script shown in Chapter 7. The four columns required are seen below in the script format.

| Slide No. | Text on the Slide. | Illustration, Photo & Audio Fx. | Storyboard (Rough sketch of the layout). |
|---|---|---|---|
| 1. | Keep text brief and succinct. | Background Image, Animation, Photograph, Drawing, Graphs, Charts, Video, and/or Audio. | Sketch Layout |
|  |  |  |  |
|  |  |  |  |
|  |  |  |  |
|  |  |  |  |
|  |  |  |  |

*Note: A multicolumn script can easily be constructed using the table function in Microsoft Word or Apple Pages. Please read the instructions in Chapter 7 and view the video online. AV script-writing programs and storyboard Apps can be used to previsualize the presentation.*

Writing the copy for a slide presentation has two parts. First is what is seen on the slide, and second is what the presenter says. There may be two scripts, one for the presenter and one for what is seen on the screen. In Apple's Keynote App, the presenter can see their script and what the audience sees projected on the screen using their computer. When traveling, it is a good idea to have a printed copy of the presenter's script in case of technical differences in connecting to local systems.

Write an outline based on the concept and subject of the presentation. The critical point is to keep the slide uncluttered with minimal text. If the audience is trying to read a lot of text on the slide, they are not listening to the speaker. The slide should complement what the speaker is saying, not duplicate it. It could be as little as one key point per slide. The slide visually represents what is being said without words. A copy of the speaker's notes can be furnished to accommodate people with hearing impairments.

The visuals on the slide must be precise. Too many elements, like charts and graphs on a slide or in a presentation, will confuse an audience. The presentation should consider who is in the audience. Is it a corporate meeting or a lecture at a university?

The pace of a slide presentation must be timed to keep everyone's attention. Once the audience reads the slide, they can become distracted if there is no new information. The speaker and the visual presentation are linked. The script for the speaker must be direct and to the point and keep pace with the slides. Keep the anecdotal stories and humor brief and engaging. The presentation's animation and short video elements will keep the audience engaged. Keep transitions between slides simple. A dissolve or cut works better than flips, wipes, or slides flying off the screen.

### Photographs and Video in Keynote
### or PowerPoint Presentations

When writing and producing a slide presentation, the venue where it will show is something to consider. Will it be projected onto large screens, monitors or seen on a laptop? Importing photographs and video clips for your presentation is easy in Keynote. The picture or clip may occupy part of the slide or the entire frame. Video clips include a bar to play and pause the clip. Video clips will also include audio if present. The more video and media are incorporated into the presentation, the bigger the file size. The larger the file size, the more memory and resources a computer needs.

If you will include photographs in your presentation, it is usually easier and better to size, crop, and prepare the pictures before bringing them into the presentation program. Pick an adequate but manageable slide show photo resolution to keep the presentation file size down. Once inserted into the slide, options are limited to basic re-sizing and positioning in the frame.

Video clips are best kept short (around two minutes maximum) because they must load and stream. The streaming rate is related to the speed of your CPU, memory, and video file size. Test the presentation on the laptop used for production to see how it handles your video clips. Clips compressed for streaming on the internet should provide the best streaming speeds for a presentation. Download the presentation from external hard drives or USB devices to an internal hard drive for maximum speeds.

Ensure your computer is connected to the projector and external PA or speakers' systems for presentations in rooms where projectors are available. You will need a video adapter to connect to a PC-based monitor or projection system when using Mac Book Pro. Portable projectors are available and worth the price if you have a large audience.

Laptop built-in speakers are small and may not convey the desired sound quality. Small portable external speakers are an option when presenting in a small conference room using only a laptop screen. Also, a remote allows you to change slides without being in front of the keyboard. When traveling, call ahead to find out what resources are available.

You can incorporate working spreadsheets and tables into a presentation. This can be an excellent tool for increasing participation by the audience and demonstrating variable concerns.

One last thought to consider as you write your presentation. More of anything is not necessarily good. Too many words and crowded slides make it challenging to read. Voice-over and effects, used in excess, can easily overwhelm the viewer.

## Audio Books

Presenting a nonfiction story using audio is a powerful way to engage and captivate listeners. Here are some critical considerations for effectively utilizing the audio medium, scriptwriting, recording techniques, editing and post-production.

### Understanding the Audio Medium

Embrace the power of sound. Audio storytelling allows you to create an immersive experience by leveraging the power of sound. Think beyond words and utilize music, ambient sounds, sound effects, and voice modulation to convey emotions, create atmosphere, and engage your audience. An audiobook can be as simple as someone reading the text. But there is the possibility of creating something more. You can adapt your written book beyond one person reading it aloud. You can also create a story that has never been in print form. We are taking the approach that whatever path you choose takes planning. Even if you plan to read and record your book aloud, you must think about how it will sound to the listener. Do you need to hire a narrator? Will reading aloud a book written to be read be the best way to present the audio version? There is a large audience for audiobooks, but is it enough to support the release of an audio version of your book?

## Limitations and Strengths

Unlike visual mediums, audio relies solely on what the listeners hear. Be mindful of this constraint and ensure your storytelling is clear, concise, and easy to follow through audio cues. Use descriptive language, vivid storytelling techniques, and well-structured narratives to engage listeners' imaginations. If there are pictures and illustrations in your book, they can be described for listeners.

Know your audience and platform: Understand the preferences and expectations of your target audience. Research the platform or medium through which your audio story will be presented (e.g., podcasts, radio, audiobooks) and tailor your approach accordingly. Consider the duration, format, and style that align with your audience's preferences.

## Scriptwriting and Recording Techniques

Craft a compelling narrative structure. Outline your nonfiction story, identifying key points, themes, and the desired flow. Develop a clear beginning, middle, and end, keeping your listeners' engagement in mind. Use storytelling techniques such as anecdotes, personal experiences, and interviews to add depth and authenticity.

Write for the spoken word. Keep your dialogue conversational and natural, as if speaking directly to your audience. Use concise sentences, avoid jargon or complex terminology, and aim for clarity. Consider using a conversational tone and engaging hooks to grab listeners' attention.

Pacing and timing are critical aspects. Be mindful of the rhythm and pacing of your audio story. Vary the pace and tone to maintain listener interest. Use pauses strategically to create dramatic impact or emphasize key points. Practice reading your script and dialogue aloud to ensure it flows smoothly.

Select the right voice talent. Consider their vocal qualities, delivery style, and ability to capture the essence of your narrative. Do you want to have a male or female narrator? If you're not recording your voice, choose a voice actor or narrator who can effectively convey the tone and style of your nonfiction story.

### Editing and Post-Production

Review and refine the recorded audio. Listen to the recorded audio carefully and identify areas needing improvement, such as clarity, pacing, or enunciation. Remove any mistakes, background noise, or technical glitches. Use audio editing software to trim, enhance, and optimize the audio quality.

Incorporate additional elements as needed. Enhance the storytelling experience by incorporating music, sound effects, or ambient sounds. Select these elements thoughtfully to complement the narrative and evoke the desired emotions.

Pay attention to pacing and transitions. Ensure the audio flows smoothly by considering the transitions between sections or segments. Use fades, crossfades, or appropriate pauses to create seamless transitions between audio elements.

Finalize the audio mix. Balance the levels of different audio elements, such as narration, music, and sound effects, to achieve a cohesive and professional sound. Adjust the volume, EQ, and other audio parameters to create a pleasant listening experience. This is best done by using a professional audio mixing engineer and facility. There are also software programs for mixing audio, like Pro Tools, that can be used if you have the experience.

Conduct a thorough quality check before publishing or sharing your audio story. Listen to the final product attentively to ensure no remaining errors, inconsistencies, or technical issues.

By understanding the audio medium, employing effective scriptwriting and recording techniques, and paying attention to editing and post-production, you can create a compelling and engaging nonfiction story that captivates listeners and brings your narrative to life.

## Converting a print book to an audiobook

Converting a print book to an audiobook involves several steps to ensure a seamless and engaging listening experience. These are the critical steps involved in the process:

Ensure you have the rights and permissions to create an audiobook version of the print book. This involves obtaining the author's consent, checking with publishers or literary agents, and addressing copyright considerations.

Adapt the print book's content into a script suitable for narration. This may involve adjusting the content for the audio medium, such as converting visual descriptions into verbal ones and rephrasing complex sentences for better auditory comprehension. Maintain the integrity of the original text while ensuring it translates well into spoken form.

### Narrator Selection

Choose a narrator suited to the book's tone, style, and subject matter. Consider their vocal qualities, delivery style, and ability to capture the essence of the narrative. Audition potential narrators or work with a professional audiobook production company that provides access to a pool of experienced voice talent.

### Recording and Production

Record the narration in a professional recording studio or a suitable acoustic environment. Ensure high-quality audio equipment is used to capture clear and crisp narration. The narrator follows the adapted script, maintaining proper pacing, tone, and expression. The production process may involve additional audio elements like music, sound effects, or chapter introductions recorded separately. Before recording, listen to the environment for a few minutes. What sounds do you hear? A book about ancient Rome doesn't need traffic and airplanes in the background, however subtle.

## Editing and Post-Production

Edit and clean up the recorded audio to remove any mistakes, background noise, or technical glitches. Ensure proper pacing and smooth transitions between segments. Adjust audio levels, EQ, and other parameters for a polished and consistent sound. Incorporate additional elements like music and sound effects as necessary.

## Quality Control and Proofing

Conduct a thorough quality check of the audiobook. Listen to the final product carefully, preferably by multiple individuals, to identify any remaining errors or inconsistencies. Address any issues found during the quality control process.

## Mastering and Formatting

Master the final audio files to ensure they meet the technical specifications for audiobook distribution platforms. Format the audiobook according to industry standards, including appropriate file formats, metadata, and chapter markers.

## Distribution and Promotion

Prepare the audiobook for distribution through various platforms such as Audible, iTunes, or other retailers. Coordinate with the appropriate channels to make the audiobook available to listeners. Develop a marketing strategy to promote the audiobook, including utilizing social media, author websites, and targeted advertising.

Throughout the process, it is essential to maintain open communication with the author, publishers, and any other relevant parties to ensure the audiobook aligns with the original print book's intent and meets everyone's expectations. Converting a print book to an audiobook requires careful attention to detail, quality production, and adherence to industry standards. By following these steps, you can successfully bring the print book to life in audio form, providing a new and immersive way for readers to experience the content. Many audiobooks have gained popularity due to their engaging content and excellent narration. Note the number of books that have narrators other than the authors.

**Best-selling audiobooks, along with their publishers:**

*"The Harry Potter Series"* by J.K. Rowling
Narrator: Stephen Fry (UK) and Jim Dale (US)
Publisher: Pottermore from J.K. Rowling/Bloomsbury
"

*Becoming"* by Michelle Obama
Narrator: Michelle Obama
Publisher: Penguin Random House Audio

*"The Martian"* by Andy Weir
Narrator: R.C. Bray
Publisher: Podium Audio

*"Born a Crime: Stories from a South African Childhood"* by Trevor Noah
Narrator: Trevor Noah
Publisher: Audible Studios

"*Where the Crawdads Sing*" by Delia Owens
Narrator: Cassandra Campbell
Publisher: Penguin Audio

"*Educated: A Memoir*" by Tara Westover
Narrator: Julia Whelan
Publisher: Random House Audio

"*The Subtle Art of Not Giving a F*ck*" by Mark Manson
Narrator: Roger Wayne
Publisher: Harper Audio

"*Atomic Habits*" by James Clear
Narrator: James Clear
Publisher: Penguin Audio

"*Sapiens: A Brief History of Humankind*"
by Yuval Noah Harari
Narrator: Derek Perkins
Publisher: Harper Audio

"*The Name of the Wind*" by Patrick Rothfuss
Narrator: Nick Podehl
Publisher: Brilliance Audio

Major audiobook publishers include Audible Studios, Penguin Random House Audio, Harper Audio, Macmillan Audio, and Simon & Schuster Audio.

An audiobooks' popularity and best-seller status can change, so it might be helpful to check contemporary lists or platforms like Audible for the most recent information.

# CHAPTER 5

# Nonfiction Publishing and Distribution

After you write your nonfiction story, there are two main ways to publish and distribute your work. The traditional route is with an established publisher. The second is by self-publishing. I had a book rejected by an established nonfiction publisher of communications books. The reason, they stated, was that my book would compete with books by their current authors. I decided to start my own publishing company and self-publish the book. I knew I had a market. Over a few years, it sold about 5000 copies through wholesalers, Amazon, and others. This is an excellent sales record for a nonfiction niche book. My company handled all aspects of publishing. Bookmasters/Baker and Taylor Publishing Services handled printing and distribution.

## Traditional Publishing

A traditional publishing house contracts with you to publish your book. Many of the following steps will be handled in-house by the publisher. You should have final approval of most steps in the process. If you choose self-publishing, you must follow up on these steps yourself. Before submitting your manuscript to a publisher, consider seeking feedback from beta readers or professional editors to refine the manuscript.

## Create a Book Proposal

Before contacting a publisher or agent, develop a compelling book proposal with an overview of your nonfiction story, target audience, market analysis, and author biography. Include a sample chapter or excerpt to give potential publishers an idea of your writing style and content.

## Research Publishing Options

Explore different publishing options, such as traditional publishing or self-publishing. Research publishers or literary agents that specialize in nonfiction and align with your story's genre or subject matter. Review submission guidelines and requirements.

## Submit to Publishers or Agents

Follow the submission guidelines provided by publishers or agents. Prepare a professional query letter or book proposal package and submit it in their preferred format (e-mail, online form, or physical mail). Be prepared for potential rejections and consider submitting to multiple publishers simultaneously. Most publishers prefer to work only with agents rather than directly with authors. Do some research to find an agent who has other nonfiction authors.

## Negotiate Publishing Contract

You will likely negotiate a publishing contract if a traditional publisher accepts your manuscript. Review the terms, royalties, and rights granted. Consider seeking legal advice to ensure the agreement aligns with your goals and interests.

## Work with an Editor

Once your manuscript is accepted, you will work closely with an editor to refine and polish your nonfiction story. The editor will provide feedback, suggest revisions, and help improve the overall quality of your work.

## Design the Book Cover and Layout

Collaborate with a professional book designer to create an eye-catching cover and an interior layout that complements your nonfiction story. Consider the visual elements, typography, and overall aesthetic that align with the book's genre and target audience.

## Print Production

Work with a reputable printer or publishing services company to produce physical copies of your book. Ensure high-quality printing, binding, and paper choices suit the genre and budget.

## Distribution and Marketing

Develop a comprehensive marketing strategy to promote your nonfiction book. Utilize various channels such as social media, author website, book signings, speaking engagements, and targeted advertising. Consider partnering with bookstores, libraries, and relevant organizations to increase visibility.

## Sales and Distribution Channels

Explore multiple sales and distribution channels to reach a wider audience. This can include online retailers like Amazon, Barnes & Noble, and independent bookstores. Consider offering your book in e-book or audiobook formats to cater to different reading preferences.

### Engage with Readers and Seek Reviews

Connect with your readers through author events, book clubs, and online platforms. Encourage readers to leave reviews on websites like Goodreads or Amazon, as positive reviews can help boost visibility and sales. Remember, the publishing industry can be competitive; success may take time and perseverance. It's crucial to continuously promote your book and engage with your target audience to build a loyal readership.

### *Self- Publishing*

Self-publishing gives authors complete control over their nonfiction stories' distribution and publishing process. It is a viable alternative to being published by an established publishing company. You can work with distributors like Amazon, Apple, or Ingram Spark. There are companies that work with authors who want to self-publish. These companies help with all aspects of self-publishing. Printing is usually "on demand." In other words, books are printed when ordered. Some publishing companies use offset printing rather than digital printing and print large quantities of books, which they either warehouse or ship to the author. There is a warehousing charge. The author is usually asked to buy a certain number of books and pay for offset printing. These companies will fill orders, receive payment, and reimburse the author minus fees and printing costs.

Authors can deal directly with bookstores like Amazon, Barnes and Noble, etc., cutting out intermediaries. To deal directly with Amazon, publish the book on KDP, in print and digital. Ingram Spark works directly with the author, prints the book, and sells it wholesale to stores, including large chains like Barnes and Noble and independent bookstores nationally and internationally. An author can choose to have Ingram Spark set up distribution with Amazon, Apple, Barnes and Noble, Target, and others. Some revenue may be lost in this scenario. Amazon also offers to set up connections to facilitate other bookstores selling a book. Independent bookstores consider Amazon a competitor. Some online services distribute on an author's behalf but may take part of the author's royalties.

An author planning to self-publish a book can be as deeply involved in all aspects of the process as they wish. Formatting the book, editing, proofreading, and designing a cover may need to be consigned to professionals in those areas. They can also be found online at "Fiverr" or "Upwork." Check freelancers' work in your area of interest to see if their style meets your needs.

### Finalize Your Manuscript

Ensure that your nonfiction story is complete, edited, and ready for publication. Proofread the content and consider hiring a professional editor to ensure quality and clarity. Find a professional editor to review your manuscript if you can afford the time and money. Rates vary depending on how much editing they do. The cost can range from about $3,000 up. Before you hire an editor, check their credentials and experience.

Obtain an International Standard Book Number (ISBN) for your book. An ISBN is a unique identifier that helps track and manage sales and distribution. You can acquire an ISBN from the appropriate agency in your country. In the U.S., Bowker sells ISBN to authors and publishers.

## Design the Book Cover and Layout

Work with a professional book designer or use self-publishing platforms that offer design tools to create an appealing book cover and interior layout. Ingram Spark and Amazon Kindle offer these services. Most platforms will furnish a template to format your book cover to the correct dimensions. Pay attention to typography, images, and overall aesthetics that reflect the genre and theme of your nonfiction story.

## Choose a Printing and Distribution Method

Decide how you will print and distribute your book. You can print-on-demand (POD) services to print copies as ordered or print a bulk quantity in advance. Research and compare different printing and distribution options to find the one that suits your needs and budget.

## Set Up an Author Account

Create an account on self-publishing platforms like Amazon Kindle Direct Publishing (KDP), Ingram Spark, Lulu, or other companies. These platforms provide tools and resources for self-publishers to upload and distribute their books in print and digital formats.

## Format Your Manuscript for Print Version

Format your manuscript according to the guidelines provided by the self-publishing platform you choose. Convert it to an appropriate file format (e.g., PDF) and ensure that it meets the specifications for printing and distribution.

## Publish Your Book

Upload your formatted manuscript, book cover, and other information to the self-publishing platform. Set the price, select the distribution channels, and choose the territories where you want your book to be available.

## Order Proof Copies

Before publishing your book, order proof copies to review the print quality, layout, and potential errors. Make any necessary revisions or corrections before finalizing the publication.

## Set Up Marketing and Promotion

Develop a marketing strategy to promote your nonfiction story. Utilize social media, author websites, e-mail newsletters, and other online channels to reach your target audience. Consider participating in virtual or physical author events, guest blogging, or seeking reviews from book bloggers and reviewers. Some platforms like Amazon and Ingram Spark have advertising and promotion options an author can use for a price. Posting notifications on social media of your book being published may bring a few sales. But most of all, it will get scores of ads offering to promote your book. Many of these offers are not worth the price.

## *Publishing the digital version*

Self-publishing the digital version of your print book allows you to reach a broader audience and offer your nonfiction story in a popular and convenient format. Here are the steps to self-publish the digital version of your print book.

## Convert Your Manuscript to a Digital Format

Prepare your manuscript in a digital format suitable for e-book publishing. The most common form is EPUB, which is widely compatible with e-readers and digital platforms. You can use tools like Calibre or professional formatting services to convert your manuscript to the appropriate format. Amazon, Barnes and Noble, and others prefer a flowable rather than a fixed format. Ingram Spark converts all EPUB submissions to a flowable format. Amazon Kindle eBooks use a unique format that works with their readers. A flowable format EPUB is converted to the Kindle format when submitted. Kindle may reject submitting a digital fixed form EPUB if it has any problems converting. Adobe InDesign can format your EPUB versions and print versions.

### Design an Eye-Catching Book Cover

Create a visually appealing book cover for your digital book. The book cover should grab potential readers' attention and accurately represent your nonfiction story's content and tone. Ensure the book cover is formatted correctly for digital platforms and looks good in thumbnail size. Most venues will furnish a template to format your book cover to the correct dimensions.

### Choose an E-Book Publishing Platform

Select self-publishing platforms for e-books, such as Amazon Kindle Direct Publishing (KDP), Apple Books, Kobo Writing Life, or Smashwords. Research each platform's requirements, royalty rates, and distribution options to find those that align with your goals. You can use more than one service to distribute an e-book.

### Format and Prepare Your E-Book

Format your manuscript specifically for e-books. Ensure proper formatting of headings, paragraphs, indents, and any images or graphs within the text. Add hyperlinks, table of contents, and metadata to enhance the reading experience. Create separate files for front matter, chapters, and back matter.

## Upload Your E-Book

Create an account on the chosen self-publishing platform and follow their guidelines to upload your e-book files. Include the cover image, book description, author bio, and relevant keywords. Set the price and select the territories where you want your e-book to be available.

## Review and Test Your E-Book

Before making your e-book available for purchase, preview it on various e-readers or use digital preview tools provided by the self-publishing platform. Check for any formatting issues, typographical errors, or layout problems. Make necessary revisions and re-upload if needed.

## Set Up Marketing and Promotion

Develop a marketing strategy to promote your e-book. Leverage social media platforms, author websites, email newsletters, and online advertising to reach your target audience. Engage with book bloggers, seek reviews, and participate in relevant online communities to increase visibility.

## Monitor Sales and Reviews

Track the sales and royalties of your e-book through the self-publishing platform's reporting tools. Monitor customer reviews and ratings and respond to reader feedback when appropriate. Utilize this feedback to improve future editions and marketing efforts.

## Explore Additional Distribution Options

Consider making your e-book available through multiple platforms to expand your reach. Some self-publishing platforms allow you to enroll your e-book in programs like Kindle Unlimited or Kindle Select, which provide additional exposure and potential earnings. Kindle may require exclusive distribution rights in certain areas.

## Update and Maintain Your E-Book

Regularly review your e-book's performance, update the content if necessary, and refresh your marketing efforts. Stay informed about industry trends and adjust your strategies accordingly to maximize the visibility and sales of your nonfiction story. Adhere to the guidelines and terms of service of the self-publishing platform you choose and comply with copyright laws and regulations. Self-publishing your digital book offers flexibility, control, and the opportunity to reach a broad audience of digital readers.

## Monitor Sales and Reviews

Keep track of your book's sales, royalties, and customer reviews through the self-publishing platform's dashboard. Monitor feedback from readers and use it to improve future editions or your marketing efforts. Self-publishing requires self-promotion and active engagement with your target audience. Continuously seek opportunities to connect with readers, collaborate with other authors, and explore marketing avenues to increase the visibility and reach of your nonfiction story.

Publishing your book independently does not guarantee financial success. There is an investment of time and money. Be aware of your priorities regarding the publishing of your book. There are millions of books on Amazon. Having it available there does not mean you will sell books. Advertising is necessary to get readers to consider buying it. Marketing can quickly become expensive. If you are self-publishing, you must do everything an established publisher would do for you. When choosing an outlet for self-publishing, consider factors such as distribution reach, royalty structures, ease of use, flexibility, and associated costs. Each platform has strengths, so you should research in-depth or consider using multiple platforms to maximize your book's visibility.

## Popular Self-publishing Outlets

- **Amazon Kindle Direct Publishing (KDP)** The most well-known platform for both eBook and print-on-demand paperbacks. Offers a vast audience, given Amazon's reach.

- *Apple Books.* For publishing eBooks on Apple's platform.Available to readers on all Apple devices.

- **Barnes & Noble Press** Allows for eBook and print-on-demand publishing. Targets the Barnes & Noble audience, especially Nook readers.

- *Kobo Writing Life.* Publishes to Kobo's vast network,which is especially prominent outside of the U.S.

- *Smashwords.* Distributes to a vast network of eBook retailers, including libraries. Allows for broader reach outside of the major platforms.

- *Draft2Digital.* Like Smashwords, distributes to a wide variety of retailers.

- Simplifies the process with tools and conversion services.

- *Lulu* Offers print-on-demand services, as well as eBook distribution. Provides options for hardcover, which some other platforms don't.

- *IngramSpark.*Known for print-on -demand, if authors want their books available in brick-and-mortar stores. Part of the larger Ingram distribution network.

- *BookBaby.* Provides comprehensive self-publishing services, including eBook conversion, cover design, and distribution. Useful for those wanting a more all-inclusive service.

- *Blurb.* Primarily known for photo books, magazines, and other visual publications. Has tools for creating professional-quality layouts.

- *Gumroad.* Best for creators selling directly to their audience. Ideal for specialized content or niche audiences.

# CHAPTER 6

## Working as a Nonfiction Writer

Working as a nonfiction writer or author offers opportunities across various types of projects, genres, and markets. There are opportunities for creative nonfiction writing in business, copywriting, and other commercial applications. Nonfiction authors write on various subjects, such as history, biographies, self-help, science, memoirs, and true crime. We'll look at a wide variety of opportunities in the nonfiction writing world.

### Magazine Articles

Write feature articles, profiles, investigative pieces, or opinion pieces for magazines covering travel, lifestyle, health, science, current affairs, and more. Many writers make a living writing specific articles for trade magazines in print and online.

### Newspaper Articles

Contribute articles to newspapers as a regular columnist, freelance journalist, or expert in a specific field. This might be doing reviews of books or movies for a local newspaper or community magazine. Stories about community people or events for local publications are also possible.

## Screenwriting

Write nonfiction scripts for documentaries, docudramas, or based-on-real-events films or television shows. Develop and write nonfiction documentary projects for film, television, streaming platforms, or online distribution.

## Content Writing

Create nonfiction content for academic publishers, including textbooks, study guides, curriculum materials, and online courses. Write content for technical publications on specific topics related to that industry.

## Translation and "Ghost Writing"

Translating nonfiction work from one language to another requires understanding both languages and the ability to write the new version without losing the meaning in the translation. There is a need for writers who can rewrite copy once it is translated into a second language in a way that feels natural. For example, suppose you are a native American English speaker and writer with Spanish as a second language. In that case, you should be more readily able to interpret a Spanish colloquialism in English. Ghost Writing is either writing the author's thoughts and ideas into a book or polishing and editing that author's writing.

## Nonfiction Genres

Nonfiction books include many disciplines and subjects. The nonfiction realm covers almost everything that isn't fictional. Going through my bookcase, I found many examples of nonfiction books. Beautiful books on art and photography, including **"Bansky,"** featuring pictures of his famous art and graffiti with commentary. **"Our America"** A photographic history by Ken Burns. Many excellent books tell their stories in words and pictures.

## Popular Nonfiction

Prevalent nonfiction crosses many disciplines. It becomes admired by making complex ideas understandable to most people. Malcolm Gladwell accomplishes this in social science with his books, including **"Outliers." "David and Goliath," "What The Dog Saw,"** and others. Nonfiction writing can be about any subject if it is factual. It can have a point of view and make a case for that opinion. The categories here are only a summary of common nonfiction areas.

## Memoirs

Share personal stories, experiences, or reflections. Auto biographical stories that focus on life experiences. **Man on a Wire**, authored by Philippe Petit with Andrew Heyl. Petit recounts six years of his life preparing to walk between the World Trade Center Towers on a wire. Many sports figures write memoirs of their time playing their sport. Often, authors writing memoirs have professional writers who help them write the book.

## Biography

Write about the lives of notable individuals, historical figures, or celebrities. Biographies require research and knowledge of the subject of the biography. A biography of Abraham Lincoln crosses over into a historical category. We have covered types of Memoirs, biographies and autobiographies in earlier chapters.

## History

Explore historical events, eras, or figures narrative or analytically. Historical facts and circumstances can be discussed in many areas, including social science, biographical, philosophical, and historical terms. The following example combines historical, political, and social elements to explore specific topical issues.

## Example

**"Caste The Origins of Our Discontents"**[1] is written in a documentary style. The words create a visual and literal narrative for the reader. The writing is clear. It tells a story that makes a historical journey through time to reveal an actuality that has been purposely ignored, swept aside, and disguised. The book's point-of-view is factual, deeply researched, and stitched together with the antidotal personal experiences of the author and many others who have experienced firsthand aspects of the American Caste system based on skin color. It may be that many of the people who blend into the dominant tier of the caste system don't consciously realize that they are part of that tier or that there is a caste system at all. But reading Caste will quickly lead to recognizing manifestations of caste wherever they reside in this multi-tiered caste system."

Author Isabel Wilkerson compares the U.S. caste system to the one in India and the one created by the Nazis in Germany under Hitler. You may be surprised to learn which system was, in part, too extreme for the Nazis to emulate in their early days completely.

### Science and Technology

Communicate scientific concepts, discoveries, or technological advancements to a general audience. The fields of science and technology offer a wide array of opportunities for nonfiction writers.

- **Science/Technology Journalism:** Writing articles for newspapers, magazines, or online platforms that

---

1 Review Caste The Origins of Our Discontents

cover recent scientific discoveries, technological advancements, or trends.

- **Technical Writing:** Crafting manuals, how-to guides, software documentation, and other materials that understandably explain complex concepts.

- **White Papers:** Producing in-depth reports on specific topics within science and technology, often used by companies to educate or persuade stakeholders.

- **Grant Writing:** Assisting researchers and organizations in writing proposals to secure funding for scientific or technological projects.

- **Book Writing:** Authoring nonfiction books on specific scientific topics, technological trends, or the biographies of prominent figures in these fields.

- **Blogging:** Creating content for blogs focusing on niche areas of science and technology, explaining concepts to laypeople and experts.

- **Corporate Communications:** Writing press releases, newsletters, and internal communications for tech companies or scientific research institutions.

- **Educational Writing:** Producing content for textbooks, e-learning platforms, or educational programs focusing on science and tech topics.

- **Science Communication (SciComm):** Bridging the gap between the scientific community and the public, making complex ideas accessible and engaging.

- **Conference & Seminar Coverage:** Attending tech conferences or scientific seminars and writing summaries, analyses, or reviews for various platforms.

- **Consulting:** *Leveraging expertise to offer insights, evaluations, or recommendations in specific areas of science and technology.*

- **Podcasting/Scriptwriting:** *Creating content for podcasts or video series that delve into topics within science and tech.*

To thrive in these opportunities, writers should prioritize accuracy, maintain curiosity, stay updated with the latest trends and discoveries, and can communicate complex ideas in an accessible and engaging manner.

**True Crime:** Investigate and present real-life crime stories, criminal cases, or forensic analysis.

**Travel Writing:** Write about travel experiences, destinations, cultures, and adventures. The travel industry provides a wealth of opportunities for nonfiction writers.

- **Travel Journalism:** *Writing articles or features for newspapers, magazines, or online platforms about destinations, trends, or travel experiences.*

- **Travel Blogging:** *Creating and maintaining a blog dedicated to personal travel experiences, destination guides, and tips.*

- **Guidebooks:** *Contributing to or authoring travel guidebooks for publishers like Lonely Planet, Fodor's, or Frommer's.*

- **Travel Memoirs:** *Penning personal travel experiences and stories in a book or essay format.*

- **Travel Photography with Captions:** *Combining evocative photography with detailed captions or* narratives, catering to visual and text-oriented audiences.

- **Hotel & Accommodation Reviews:** Providing in-depth analysis or reviews of hotels, hostels, or other accommodation types for various platforms.

- **Airline & Cruise Writing:** Reviewing or detailing experiences on airlines, cruises, or other modes of travel.

- **Travel Gear Reviews:** Writing reviews or guides on the latest travel gear and gadgets.

- **Cultural Essays:** Producing in-depth essays on specific destinations' cultures, traditions, or histories.

- **Travel News Reporting:** Covering the latest news or trends in the travel industry.

- **Destination Marketing:** Collaborating with tourism boards or travel companies to produce promotional content about destinations or services.

- **Travel Itineraries:** Crafting detailed trip itineraries for various audiences, from luxury travelers to backpackers.

- **Travel Newsletters:** Curating or creating content for regular newsletters dedicated to travel enthusiasts.

- **Travel Workshops & Seminars:** Leading or participating in workshops on travel writing, photography, or related skills.

To succeed in the travel writing field, writers should prioritize authentic storytelling, cultural sensitivity, thorough research, and a genuine passion for exploring. Building a solid portfolio and establishing industry connections can help secure more opportunities.

**Self-Help and Personal Development:** Provide guidance, advice, and strategies for personal growth, success, or well-being. Self-Help and Personal Development: Provide guidance, advice, and strategies for personal growth, success, or well-being. The fields of self-help and personal development are vast and offer numerous opportunities for nonfiction writers.

- **Self-help Books:** Writing full-length books offering advice, strategies, or insights on personal growth, mindset, or life skills.

- **Blogging:** Maintaining a blog dedicated to self-improvement topics, sharing personal experiences, lessons, and actionable advice.

- **Article Contributions:** Writing articles for magazines, newspapers, or online platforms focusing on personal development topics.

- **E-books & Guides:** Creating shorter digital books or guides on specific topics, such as stress management, goal setting, or time management.

- **Workshops & Seminars:** Crafting content for or leading workshops and seminars on personal development techniques or strategies.

- **Online Courses:** Designing and scripting content for e-learning platforms offering self-help courses.

- **Affirmation & Meditation Scripts:** Writing guided meditations or affirmation scripts for use in apps, recordings, or live sessions.

- **Webinars:** Hosting or scripting online sessions that tackle specific self-improvement subjects.

- **Podcasting/Scriptwriting**: Creating content for podcasts that delve into self-help themes, interviews with experts, or motivational stories.

- **Journals & Planners:** Designing content for guided journals or planners that help individuals track and progress in their personal development journey.

- **Consulting & Coaching:** Personal consultations or coaching sessions, including writing personalized plans, guides, or client resources.

- **Newsletters:** Curating or crafting content for regular newsletters focused on motivation, personal growth tips, or the latest findings in the field.

- **Collaborations:** Teaming with influencers, YouTubers, or public figures to co-write books, produce courses, or develop other content.

To thrive in self-help and personal development, writers should prioritize authenticity, continuous personal growth, research-backed methods, and a genuine passion for helping others. Building trust with readers or listeners is crucial, so combining unique experiences with evidence-based advice often resonates best.

## Blogs and Online Publications

Create content for your blog or other blogs. Contribute articles to online publications covering various topics and niches.

**Writing for Blogs:** Online blogs accept articles on subjects relating to their themes. Submissions are usually less than 800 words. There are many opportunities for writers who are interested in writing for blogs:

- **Guest Blogging:** Many blogs accept guest posts, allowing writers to share their expertise and perspectives. This gives the writer exposure and can lead to paid opportunities.

- **Freelance Blogging:** Websites like Upwork, Freelancer, and ProBlogger Job Board frequently list blogging gigs. Writers can pitch their services and get hired for one-off or ongoing blog writing tasks.

- **Affiliate Blogging:** Writers can create content promoting products and earn a commission for every sale through their referral links.

- **In-house Blogger for Companies:** Many companies maintain blogs to connect with their audience and improve their online presence. Writers can find opportunities as salaried or contract bloggers.

- **Blogging Networks:** Some blogging networks pay writers to contribute content on various topics. Examples from the past include HubPages and the now-defunct Yahoo! Voices.

- **Personal Blogs:** Writers can start their blogs around niches they're passionate about. With consistent quality content and effective marketing, they can monetize their blogs through advertising, sponsored posts, or selling products.

- **Content Agencies:** These agencies produce content for a variety of clients. Joining one can provide consistent work, as they often need multiple daily or weekly blog posts.

- **Niche Expertise:** Writers with expertise in specific fields (e.g., technology, health, finance) can find opportunities on blogs that focus on those niches.

- **Collaborative Blogging Platforms:** Websites like Medium allow writers to share content and earn money based on engagement and readership.

- **Sponsored Posts:** As a recognized blogger or influencer, companies might approach writers to review or promote their products/services in exchange for payment.

While many opportunities exist, building a reputation for quality and reliability is critical to long-term success in blogging.

**Pod Casts:** Writers are needed to script podcasts on a diverse number of nonfiction subjects. The podcasting world offers numerous opportunities for writers and scriptwriters.

- **Scriptwriting** for Narrative Podcasts: Much like TV shows or movies, many podcasts have scripted narratives, often in genres like drama, mystery, or sci-fi. Writers can craft these stories independently or as part of a team.

- **Research and Scriptwriting for Non-fiction Podcasts:** Shows that delve into history, science, or true crime, for instance, require writers to research and script episodes that are both factual and engaging.

- **Commercial Scriptwriting:** As podcasts grow in popularity, so does advertising on them. Writers can craft compelling ad scripts tailored for podcast audiences.

- **Collaboration with Hosts:** Some podcast hosts aren't writers but are experts in their fields. They might collaborate with writers to structure their episodes and draft outlines or scripts.

- **Show Notes and Descriptions:** Podcasts usually have detailed notes, providing summaries, links, and additional information. Writers can specialize in creating these concise yet informative notes.

- **Consultation for Podcasters:** Experienced writers can offer consultation services to new podcasters, helping them hone their voices, structure their content, and develop their show's narrative arc.

- **Transcriptions:** While this isn't "writing" in the traditional sense, transcribing podcasts can be a lucrative opportunity. It makes content accessible and can improve a podcast's SEO.

- **Development of Spin-off Content:** A popular podcast can spawn eBooks, blog posts, or even physical books. Writers can be tasked with adapting or expanding upon podcast content for these mediums.

- **Piloting Original Concepts:** Writers can develop their podcast concepts, creating pilots or series proposals to pitch to podcast networks or independent producers.

- **Interactive Podcasts:** With the rise of interactive audio experiences (e.g., choose-your-own-adventure style narratives), writers can craft branching scripts that allow listeners to choose the story's direction.

To tap into these opportunities, writers should be familiar with the unique demands and nuances of the audio medium, understand the importance of pacing, and be adaptable to changes based on production needs and feedback.

### Television and Radio

Write for nonfiction television and radio programs, including documentaries, reality shows, or news segments. This is specialized writing for various subjects. Writing for television and radio often includes writing copy that is meant to be spoken.

Broadcast radio, despite being one of the oldest forms of mass media, remains a potent platform for nonfiction writers seeking to disseminate their work to a broad audience. With the vast array of talk shows, news segments, documentaries, and feature programs, there is a persistent demand for engaging, fact-based content. Writers can explore topics ranging from current events, biographical sketches, and cultural commentaries to in-depth investigations. This medium offers a unique challenge: to convey information compellingly using only sound, without the visual aids that television or online platforms provide.

Write and develop nonfiction scripts for documentary films, biopics, or adaptations of actual events. For independent production or television. Write nonfiction content for cable networks specializing in documentary programming or factual entertainment.

Develop nonfiction materials for academic publishers, including textbooks, e-learning platforms, and educational websites. Write nonfiction content for public relations campaigns, corporate publications, or content marketing initiatives.

It's important to note that the specific markets and opportunities may vary based on location, industry trends, and personal connections. Stay updated with industry news, network with professionals, and adapt your skills and writing style to cater to different markets and genres to maximize your opportunities as a nonfiction writer or author.

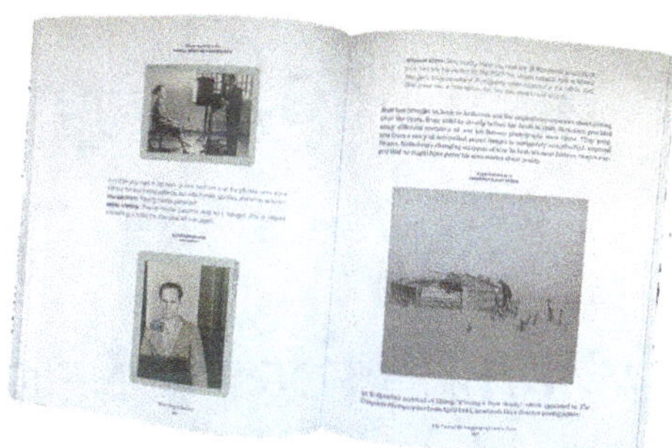

Study of photographic intricacies and actuality page layout.

"From hard-hitting investigative pieces to enlightening self-help guides, the expansive world of nonfiction awaits the curious writer."

"Unveiling truths, sharing expertise, or sparking inspiration — a writer's canvas in the vast realm of nonfiction books."

CHAPTER **7**

# WRITING FOR NONFICTION FILM AND VIDEO

Creating a nonfiction story using video or film is an engaging way to convey information and capture the audience's attention. This type of story is often a documentary, educational, or nonfiction program for television. The same principles for writing a nonfiction book can be translated into visual approaches in film, video, and photographic nonfiction work. A documentary project must have a shooting script that creates a visual narrative that can be shot and edited into a complete story. The opportunity exists to use the visual medium to develop descriptive language that engages the viewer in the story narrative. Film and video rely on action to move the story along. Instead of words, paragraphs, and chapters, there are shots, dialogue, narration, and scenes. Here are some critical aspects to consider when writing for visual and audio recording mediums.

## Visual Presentation and Storytelling

- *Video allows you to use visual elements such as footage, images, graphics, and animations to convey your nonfiction story. Visuals have the potential to enhance and create the narrative.*

- Video storytelling has a rhythm and pacing. Be mindful of the duration and pace of your video to maintain viewer engagement. Consider the appropriate length for your target audience and platform.

- Audio considerations: Audio plays a crucial role in video storytelling. Pay attention to sound quality, including clear narration or interviews, background music, and appropriate use of sound effects. Ensure a balanced audio mix that complements the visuals.

## Scriptwriting and Storyboarding

- Develop a clear narrative structure: Outline your nonfiction story and identify the key points, themes, and desired flow. Craft a compelling beginning, middle, and end that engages viewers. Ensure your script communicates the story effectively and aligns with your objectives.

- Write for visuals and spoken word: Your script should complement the visuals, incorporating descriptive language and engaging dialogue or narration. Consider the timing of visuals and audio, allowing them to work together to convey the message.

- Storyboarding: Create a visual roadmap of your video using storyboards. Sketch out each scene or shot, indicating camera angles, movements, and the sequence of visuals. Storyboarding helps visualize the final product and ensures a cohesive and well-structured video.

## Framing and Composition

- Review the visual design of each shot. Use the rule of thirds, leading lines, and depth of field to create visually appealing and balanced images. Experiment with different angles, perspectives, and camera movements to add depth and interest.

- Visual storytelling elements incorporate images that support and enhance the narrative. Use close-ups, wide shots, or cutaways to focus on crucial details, convey emotions, or provide context. Consider incorporating relevant B-roll footage, archival material, or graphics to enhance the storytelling.

- Pay attention to lighting and aesthetic conditions to ensure clear and well-lit shots. Consider the mood and aesthetics you want to convey through lighting and color choices. Use lighting techniques to create depth and highlight essential elements.

## Nonfiction Script Writing[1]

"A shooting script for a documentary does not "script" what the subject will do or say. It details what the filmmakers will do and the questions that will be asked. In some cases where there will be a voice-over narrator, the script will show what the narration might be and the picture that goes with it. But this narration may change in the final editing script once the footage has been obtained. First-person interviews will be used in certain scenes instead of the voice-over narrator. "

"The shooting script for a documentary is a guide to shooting, a wish list in some ways, for action that fits the vision for that scene. Some scripted images may not be obtainable, while other opportunities might present themselves as shooting progresses. The shooting script is the basis for getting the coverage necessary to tell the story. It is also needed to determine the equipment and crew required for scheduling and budget considerations."

"Formats for nonfiction film scripts and documentaries differ from those for theatrical fiction film screenplays. A

---

1 Chapter 3-138 Documentary Directing and Storytelling – James R. Martin

basic two-column script with a column for the picture and a column for the audio is used. A column for the shot number and one for the approximate time of the shot may be added. This format works as a shooting script or an editing script. It sometimes has another column in nonfiction production for a storyboard picture or photograph."

## How to Format a Multi-column Shooting or Editing Script[2]

SHOOTING SCRIPT

| SHOT | PICTURE | TIME | AUDIO |
|---|---|---|---|
| 1 | CU Farmer's face | :05 | Ambient Sound - VO from interview. |
| 2 | LS Farmer walking toward barn | :07 | Ambient Sound - VO from interview |
| 3 | MS Farmer **Bob Longwell** standing next to row of Dairy Cows. [super name lower 3'] | :10 | Interview continues: Answer to question – Why did you become a Dairy Farmer? |
| 4 | | | |

"The multi-column script format may be used for any documentary or nonfiction project. This includes industrial, corporate, educational, sales, commercial, informational film, video, or multimedia projects. Using the "landscape" rather than "portrait" layout allows for additional columns to be added for the storyboard or other information.

Include the event activities and the subject's actions in the script if they are predictable. Include any details known about the environment or action.

2  Chapter 3-139 Documentary Directing and Storytelling – James R. Martin

A multi-column script is formatted using the "table" drop-down menu in Microsoft Word®. Creating the script with the "table" menu produces a multiple-column script in which the cells in each row expand simultaneously so that Picture and Audio frames stay next to each other in the same row.

Pick the number of columns (four) and rows. Ten is good. More rows can always be added by tabbing on the last cell to add another row. Size your columns by dragging the lines to where you want them."

### Video Tutorial – Formatting a Nonfiction multicolumn script.

**For a short video on formatting a multicolumn script using Microsoft Word® go to: https://www.youtube.com/watch?v=vCApfQOglZs&t=66s**

### Editing and Post-Production

Assembly and sequencing: Organize your footage and visuals according to your script and storyboard. Arrange the

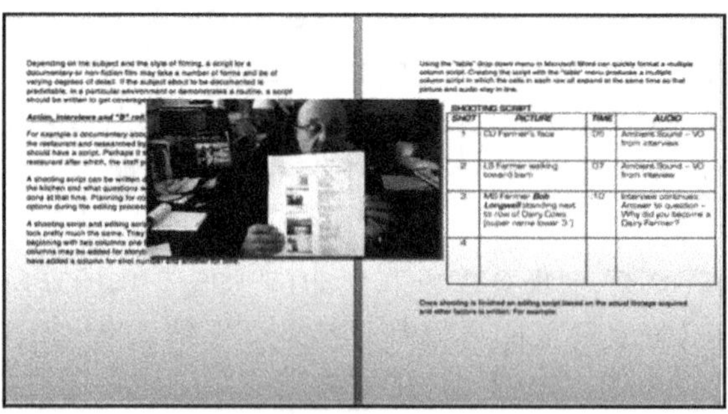

shots in a logical sequence to create a cohesive narrative.

Consider the timing of transitions and pacing between scenes.

Enhancing the storytelling: Use editing techniques such as cuts, transitions, overlays, and visual effects to enhance the storytelling. Ensure smooth transitions between shots and maintain a consistent visual and audio flow.

Incorporating audio and music: Edit the audio elements, including narration, interviews, and sound effects, to synchronize with the visuals. Select appropriate background music or ambient sounds to enhance the mood and reinforce the narrative.

Color grading and visual enhancements: Apply color grading techniques to achieve a consistent and visually appealing look throughout the video. Enhance the visuals through color correction, contrast adjustments, and other post-production techniques.

Finalizing and exporting: Review the edited video for improvements or corrections. Once satisfied, export the video in the appropriate format and resolution for the intended platform or distribution channels.

Understand the medium you are working with. Write a solid script and storyboard. By applying effective editing and post-production techniques, you can create a compelling nonfiction story that engages and captivates your audience visually and emotionally.

# Adapting a nonfiction print book to film or video.

Adapting a nonfiction print work to film or video involves carefully translating the content effectively to be presented visually. A critical aspect of adapting a nonfiction work to the screen is keeping the film or video in the nonfiction genre. Recreating historical events for the video may be acceptable in some instances. But doing so will move the story into a hybrid nonfiction genre. Here are the steps in adapting a nonfiction print work to a movie or video.

## Understand the Source Material

Read and analyze the nonfiction print work thoroughly to grasp its core themes, narrative structure, and critical messages. Identify the most compelling elements that can be visualized effectively. Research imagery that can match the book's descriptions and locations.

## Identify the Target Audience and Purpose

Determine the intended audience for the adapted film or video. Study how the content can be tailored to engage and resonate with the target audience. Clarify whether the adaptation's purpose is educational, informative, or entertaining.

## Outline and Structure the Adaptation

Develop an outline or treatment that maps out the print work's key points, themes, and scenes. Identify the most critical sections or chapters to include how they will be presented visually. Decide on any necessary modifications to the structure to suit the visual storytelling format.

## Write a Script

Write a script that translates the nonfiction content into a visual narrative. Adapt the written material into dialogue, action sequences, and graphic descriptions. Ensure that the script captures the essence of the source material while taking advantage of the film/video medium. If the story is to remain in the nonfiction realm, it must use actuality visual material. Interviews with individuals or experts can be used to convey critical aspects of the book's themes.

## Visualize and Storyboard

Create visual representations of each scene or sequence through storyboards. Sketch out each scene's key shots, camera angles, and compositions. This helps in visualizing the adaptation and planning of the production process.

## Pre-production Planning

Prepare for the production by organizing logistics, such as scouting locations, assembling a production team, casting actors or interviewees, and acquiring necessary permits or rights. Create a production schedule and budget to ensure a smooth production process.

## Production

Shoot the scenes and sequences as planned in the script and storyboards. Shoot high-quality footage, conduct interviews if required, and ensure proper lighting, sound recording, and camera techniques. Stay true to the visualized adaptation while allowing for creative flexibility during filming.

## Post-production

Edit the captured footage to assemble the final film or video. This includes selecting the best takes, arranging scenes, adding transitions, incorporating visual effects or animations if needed, and enhancing the audio quality. Edit the content to maintain a cohesive and engaging narrative.

## Sound Design and Music

Add sound effects and background music to enhance the storytelling and create a more immersive experience. Ensure that the audio elements complement the visuals and help convey the intended emotions and atmosphere.

## Finalize and Distribute

Review and refine the edited film or video to ensure its coherence, clarity, and quality. Seek feedback from trusted individuals or focus groups. Once satisfied, finalize the project, and export it in the appropriate format for distribution across various platforms, such as film festivals, online streaming, or educational channels.

Throughout the adaptation process, it's essential to maintain the source material's integrity while leveraging the visual medium's strengths to engage and captivate the audience. Collaborate with a dedicated team of professionals, including directors, cinematographers, editors, and sound designers, to successfully bring the adaptation to life.

## Examples of cinematic nonfiction storytelling.

**"The Thin Blue Line" (1988)** - directed by Errol Morris, this documentary tells the story of Randall Dale Adams, a man wrongly convicted of murder in Texas. Morris uses a mix of interviews, reenactments, and cinematic techniques to construct a compelling narrative that challenges the official version of events.

**"Hoop Dreams" (1994)** - directed by Steve James, this documentary follows the lives of two high school basketball players from inner-city Chicago as they pursue their dreams of playing in the NBA. James uses a fly-on-the-wall approach to capture the boys' lives and constructs a powerful narrative that explores race, class, and opportunity issues.

**"Man on Wire" (2008)** - directed by James Marsh, this documentary tells the story of Philippe Petit, a French high-wire artist who walked between the Twin Towers of the World Trade Center in 1974. Marsh uses a mix of archival footage, interviews, and reenactments to construct a suspenseful and emotional narrative that explores Petit's motivations and the cultural significance of his feat.

**"Amy" (2015)** - directed by Asif Kapadia, this documentary tells the story of Amy Winehouse, the British singer-songwriter who died tragically in 2011 at 27. Kapadia uses a mix of archival footage, interviews, and home videos to construct a powerful and intimate portrait of Winehouse, exploring her struggles and the pressures of fame.

**"Wrapped In Steel"** (1984) is a documentary film directed by James R. Martin, the author of this book, with cinematographer and co-editor Michael Goi. The film explores the history and culture of a working-class neighborhood, the American steel industry, and its impact on the lives of steelworkers and their families. Through interviews with current and former steelworkers, as well as archival footage and photographs, the film provides a powerful and emotional look at the history of the Chicago neighborhood and this vital industry.

The film is structured around the story of multiple families of steelworkers of different ethnic backgrounds and their experiences working in the industry and living in the Southeast Chicago neighborhood. The worker's stories are used to explore the film's broader themes, including the decline of the American steel industry, the impact of globalization on the industry and its workers, and the struggle for workers' rights and safety. The documentary also includes interviews with experts in the field of labor and industry, as well as politicians and community leaders, providing a well-rounded and informative view of the subject.

Overall, "Wrapped In Steel" is a well-made and compelling documentary that provides a valuable perspective on an essential industry in American history. It sheds light on the challenges steelworkers and their families face and the impact of the industry's decline on communities nationwide. It also explores life in the multi-ethnic, multi-racial neighborhoods comprising the Southeast side of Chicago until 1984, when the documentary aired nationally on Public Television in the U.S.

The PBS documentary series **"Civil War"** (1990), directed by Ken Burns, is an iconic and highly acclaimed portrayal of one of the most significant events in American history. Comprising nine episodes, the series delves deep into the causes, progression, and aftermath of the American Civil War, which lasted from 1861 to 1865. Using a combination of archival photographs, personal letters, diary entries, and expert interviews, Burns weaves together a comprehensive narrative that brings to life the complexities and human stories of the war. The series explores the political divisions, the experiences of soldiers and civilians, the social and economic impact, and the profound changes that occurred during this pivotal period in American history.

Through meticulous research and attention to detail, "Civil War" offers a nuanced understanding of the conflict, shedding light on the motivations, struggles, and ideologies that shaped the war's course. It examines the perspectives of the Union and Confederate sides, providing a balanced portrayal of the key figures, battles, and moments that defined the era.

Beyond the military aspects, the series delves into broader societal issues, including slavery, emancipation, and the quest for equality. It also explores the war's impact on American identity and its enduring legacy on the nation.

Ken Burns' signature storytelling style, characterized by slow panning shots, evocative music, and the use of primary source materials, lends a sense of intimacy and emotional depth to the series. "Civil War" is widely regarded as a seminal work in documentary filmmaking, offering an engrossing and comprehensive exploration of the complexities and consequences of the American Civil War.

These examples demonstrate how nonfiction storytelling can be used in cinema to construct compelling narratives that explore important issues and engage audiences on an emotional level. They use various techniques, including interviews, reenactments, and archival footage, to create a sense of immediacy and intimacy that draws the viewer in. These same methods are used for written nonfiction storytelling. Documentaries and nonfiction films and videos rely on strong written concepts, treatments, shooting scripts, and editing scripts.

# Writing a Nonfiction Game Story

Writing a nonfiction story for a digital game can be a unique and immersive experience. Writers of nonfiction game stories, which recount actual events within the context of a game or interactive setting, require a unique set of qualifications. They must firmly grasp narrative techniques to craft compelling stories while maintaining factual accuracy. Familiarity with the gaming industry, history, and current trends ensures authenticity and relatability. Excellent research skills are crucial for gathering and verifying information, providing that events, dates, and details align with actual occurrences.

Additionally, writers should be adept at interactive storytelling techniques, understanding the nuances of player agency while staying true to real-life narratives. Collaboration skills are also essential, as these writers often work closely with game developers, designers, and other stakeholders to ensure the seamless integration of factual narratives within gameplay mechanics. Here are some steps to consider when crafting a nonfiction story for a digital game.

### Define Your Objective

Determine the purpose of your nonfiction story within the game. Is it to educate, inspire, entertain, or a combination of these? Clarify the main message or takeaway you want players to experience through the story.

### Research and Gather Information

Conduct thorough research on your chosen nonfiction topic. Collect relevant facts, historical events, real-world locations, and other elements that will form the basis of your story. Ensure that the information is accurate and well-documented.

### Identify the Gameplay Mechanics

Understand the gameplay mechanics and features of the digital game. Consider how the story can be integrated into the gameplay experience. Determine how player choices and interactions can influence the narrative or outcome.

### Develop the Story Structure

Outline the key elements and structure of your nonfiction story. Determine the main story arc, characters, and their motivations. Consider incorporating real-life events, people, or scenarios that align with the nonfiction theme. Identify the potential conflicts and challenges that players will face.

### Write Engaging Dialogue and Narratives

Write dialogue that reflects the voices and personalities of the characters. Write narratives that blend information with compelling storytelling. Use descriptive language, vivid imagery, and engaging dialogue to immerse players in the nonfiction world.

### Create Interactive Elements

Explore ways to make the nonfiction story interactive within the game. Incorporate choices, branching paths, and consequences that allow players to engage with the narrative and shape their experience. Balance interactivity with the need to convey essential information or historical accuracy.

## Integrate Gameplay and Story

Ensure seamless integration of the nonfiction story with gameplay mechanics. Create moments where the story influences gameplay, such as puzzles, challenges, or missions based on actual events. Strive for a cohesive, immersive experience that encourages players to explore and engage with the story.

## Test and Iterate

Test the nonfiction story within the game to gather feedback from playtesters. Evaluate how the story elements impact the gameplay experience and adjust accordingly. Iterate on the dialogue, pacing, or interactive features to enhance player engagement and enjoyment.

## Enhance with Multimedia Elements

Consider incorporating multimedia elements such as images, videos, or audio recordings to enrich the nonfiction story. These elements can provide additional context, historical references, or real-life testimonials to deepen players' understanding and connection with the narrative.

## Ensure Accessibility and Usability

Pay attention to accessibility features and ensure that a wide range of people can enjoy the nonfiction story. Provide clear instructions, tooltips, or in-game prompts to guide players through the story. Consider subtitles or localization options to make the content accessible to diverse audiences. Writing a nonfiction story for a digital game requires a balance between factual accuracy, engaging storytelling, and interactive gameplay. Collaborate with game designers, developers, and other team members to ensure that the nonfiction elements seamlessly integrate with the game mechanics, creating a captivating and educational experience for players. Interactive storytelling with historical or real-world contexts offers an engaging gameplay experience and a reflection on past or present realities. Games can offer a blend of education, storytelling, and interactivity, engaging players while providing insights into real-world topics.

## A Few Digital Nonfiction Games

- *"Never Alone (Kisima Innitchuna)" by Upper One Games and E-Line Media. This game delves into the indigenous stories of the Iñupiaq people of Alaska. With a mix of platforming and puzzles, players experience traditional tales, all narrated in the Iñupiaq language.*

- *"That Dragon, Cancer" by Numinous Games. A touching and emotional narrative-driven game that tells the real-life story of a family dealing with their young son's terminal cancer diagnosis.*

- *A Short Hike" by Adam Robinson-Yu. While it's a blend of fiction and nonfiction, the game captures the therapeutic essence of nature hikes and explores the concept of personal growth and overcoming obstacles.*

- *"Zoo Tycoon" series by Blue Fang Games (original). Players manage and build a zoo. The game teaches about different animal species, their habitats, and their needs.*

- This War of Mine" by 11-bit studios. Based on the actual experiences of people living in war-torn cities, this game allows players to control a group of civilians trying to survive in a city under siege.

- "Valiant Hearts: The Great War" by Ubisoft Montpellier. Tells the story of four characters during World War I and is interwoven with actual letters from the front lines. It gives a touching and educational perspective on the Great War

C H A P T E R **8**

# Writing for Distribution of Nonfiction Films and Videos

Navigating the multifaceted landscape of distributing visual nonfiction work requires writers to be well-versed in various strategies and distribution channels. These channels, from digital streaming platforms to physical exhibition spaces like museums or galleries, have unique requirements and audiences. A nuanced understanding of these channels is imperative for writers, as it directly influences the creation of practical material. This material might include detailed descriptions that vividly convey visual content, concise synopses that capture the essence of a work, comprehensive summaries providing an in-depth overview, persuasive pitches targeting potential investors or collaborators, and meticulously crafted submission documents tailored for film festivals or distribution networks. By mastering the intricacies of these various types of content, writers can effectively bridge the gap between visual creators and their intended audience, ensuring the work's reach and impact.

There are diverse strategies and distribution channels for the distribution of visual nonfiction work. Writers must understand these distribution techniques to write various types of material such as descriptions, synopsis, summaries, pitches, and submission documents for festivals and distribution.

## Film Festivals

Submit your work to relevant film festivals focusing on documentary content. Film festivals provide a platform for exposure, networking opportunities, and potential recognition for your work. Research and target festivals that align with your genre, subject matter, or themes.

## Theatrical Release

You may consider a theatrical release if your nonfiction film has commercial potential or a significant audience appeal. Work with independent theaters or art-house cinema venues that showcase documentary films. Develop a marketing and distribution strategy to attract audiences to the theaters.

## Broadcast and Cable Television

Approach television networks, cable channels, or streaming platforms that broadcast nonfiction or documentary content. Pitch your film to broadcasters or distributors who specialize in this genre. Negotiate licensing agreements or distribution deals to have your movie aired on television or made available through streaming services.

## Sample submissions or "pitch" processes.

Submitting nonfiction or documentary work to streaming platforms like Netflix or HBO typically involves a formal submission process. While the specific procedures and requirements may vary, here are some general guidelines.

## Netflix Submission Process

Research and understand Netflix's content needs. Familiarize yourself with the types of nonfiction or documentary content that Netflix is interested in acquiring. Visit their website, read industry news, and study their existing catalog to gain insights into their programming preferences. Netflix's priorities change depending on their assessment of what viewers are watching and the availability of products. Nonfiction programming is less popular than fiction.

Find a distributor or production company (Optional). Netflix often acquires content through distribution or production companies. Consider partnering with a reputable distributor or production company experienced in pitching and negotiating deals with streaming platforms like Netflix. Netflix prefers to deal with registered agents.

## Prepare a Pitch Package

Create a comprehensive pitch package that showcases your nonfiction or documentary work. It should include the following.

- *A compelling synopsis or logline that highlights the unique aspects of your project.*

- *A detailed treatment or outline that outlines the story, themes, and approach.*

- *Information about the director, producers, and critical talent involved.*

- *Sample footage or a trailer demonstrating your work's visual and storytelling quality.*

- *Any relevant awards, accolades, or notable festival screenings.*

## Submit Your Pitch

Submit your pitch package through Netflix's official website or online submission portal if one is available. Alternatively, if you have partnered with a distributor or production company, they may handle the submission process on your behalf.

## HBO Submission Process

Research HBO's Content Needs: Understand HBO's programming focus and the types of nonfiction or documentary content they seek. Review their website, programming lineup, and any specific guidelines they provide for submissions.

Prepare a Pitch Package: Create a comprehensive pitch package that effectively communicates the essence of your nonfiction or documentary work.

- *The package should include a clear and concise synopsis or logline that captures the essence of your project.*
- *A detailed treatment or outline that highlights your work's story, themes, and unique aspects.*
- *Information about the director, producers, and critical talent involved.*
- *Sample footage or a trailer showcasing your work's visual and storytelling quality.*
- *Any relevant awards, accolades, or notable festival screenings.*

Submit Your Pitch: HBO typically accepts submissions through established production companies or through agents. It is less common for them to accept unsolicited submissions directly from filmmakers. Therefore, partnering with a reputable production company or securing representation is advisable to pitch your project to HBO.

Networking and Industry Connections: Building relationships within the industry, attending film festivals, and connecting with professionals in the documentary or nonfiction field can increase your chances of getting noticed by HBO or receiving recommendations for submission.

Remember that the submission process and requirements can change over time, so it's essential to regularly check the respective websites or contact the platforms directly for the most up-to-date information. Additionally, consider seeking legal advice or consulting with industry professionals to ensure you understand the terms and conditions of any potential distribution deals before proceeding.

## Video-on-Demand (VOD) Platforms

Make your nonfiction film available on popular VOD platforms like Amazon Prime Video, Netflix, Hulu, Vimeo on Demand, or iTunes. These platforms provide a global reach and accessibility to a broad audience. Research their submission processes and guidelines to include your film in their catalog.

## Educational Distribution

Target educational institutions, libraries, and organizations focusing on nonfiction or documentary education. Develop partnerships with distributors specializing in academic content. This allows your film to be used for educational purposes in classrooms, workshops, or training programs.

### Online Platforms and Websites

Create your website or utilize video-sharing platforms like YouTube or Vimeo to showcase your nonfiction work. Build an online presence, engage with your audience, and use social media to promote and share your film. Consider monetizing your content through advertising, sponsorships, or crowdfunding.

### DVD Sales and Merchandise

Produce DVDs or Blu-rays of your nonfiction film and sell them directly through your website or at screenings and events. Create merchandise like posters, books, or limited-edition items related to your movie to generate additional revenue and enhance the fan experience.

### Non-Theatrical Screenings

Organize non-theatrical screenings at community centers, universities, museums, or other venues. Collaborate with organizations, activists, or interest groups related to your film's subject matter to organize screenings and discussions.

### International Distribution

Explore opportunities for international distribution by partnering with international distributors or attending film markets and festivals focusing on global distribution. Understand different regions' cultural and legal requirements to ensure proper allocation and licensing.

### Do it yourself (DIY) and Self-Distribution

Consider self-distribution if you prefer to maintain complete control over the distribution process. This involves directly selling or renting your film through your website, organizing screenings, and fulfilling orders yourself. While this approach requires more effort and marketing, it provides greater autonomy and potential financial returns.

Consider your nonfiction work's target audience and tailor your distribution strategy accordingly. Creating a comprehensive marketing plan, including publicity, press releases, social media campaigns, and networking within the industry, is essential. Distributing your nonfiction film requires persistence, adaptability, and a strategic approach to reach the broadest possible audience and maximize its impact.

# Chapter 9

## Case Study

## Writing and Publishing: Insights from "Documentary Directing and Storytelling" Book.

### Back Story

My first foray into publishing was not with "Documentary Directing and Storytelling" but with "Create Documentary Films, Videos, and Multimedia." This book evolved from my lecture notes, presentation materials, and a handbook crafted for my documentary filmmaking course. Subtitled as "a comprehensive guide to documentary storytelling techniques for various media," Focal Press expressed interest in it. However, they found it, too, like the works of several other authors in their roster. As a solution, I established Real Deal Press and partnered with a printing and distribution company to publish the book in 2010. Over the next five years, it sold around 4000 copies in its role as a textbook. While I initially considered revising this book after its "Revised Third Edition," I realized I wanted to dissect specific areas like Nonfiction Storytelling, Directing, Editing, Writing, Cinematography, Producing, and Distributing – all topics touched upon in the original.

## Writing Process

The journey of "Documentary Directing and Storytelling" began by extrapolating content on directing from "Create Documentary Films, Videos, and Digital Media." I aimed to delve deeper into the nuances of directing documentaries and other nonfiction works. I mined material from the previous book, updated it, and integrated it seamlessly into the new job. Additionally, I enriched the content using materials from my Documentary Filmmaking Course, incorporating photographs, illustrations, and practical examples.

Upon completing the first draft, I proofread and edited, compiling a bibliography, a filmography, and an index – elements collectively called the "Backmatter." The "Frontmatter," encompassing the title pages, copyright details, disclaimers, acknowledgments, table of contents, foreword, and preface, was slated for completion once the main content was in place. While I had the elements of the Frontmatter written, they hadn't been integrated into the InDesign chapter.

## Designing the Book

Transitioning a manuscript into a publish-ready format requires the right tools. Adobe InDesign is often hailed as the gold standard for this. The initial step involves selecting a template – either custom-made or purchased. I opted for a pre-designed one from Book Design Templates, driven by their competitive pricing and comprehensive user instructions. However, integrating the template with InDesign and subsequently pouring the manuscript into the template proved to be more intricate than anticipated. One valuable insight was the inefficacy of importing an extensive manuscript with numerous chapters as a singular file. Instead, the optimal approach was configuring InDesign for a 'Book' setup and introducing each chapter individually. Although I adjusted the text while formulating it in InDesign, the platform isn't conducive for post-adjustment proofreading or editing, especially given its limitations in detecting grammatical or stylistic discrepancies. Its primary function remains book construction, like determining the print dimensions and formatting.

### Editing and Proofreading

It took nearly a year to complete a publish-ready book. I cannot emphasize enough the importance of having your work reviewed by a professional editor. While publishers typically provide editorial services, self-publishing authors might need help critically assessing their writing. If budget constraints prevent hiring an editor, switch to an editorial mindset, meticulously reviewing your content. Having a trusted individual critique, the manuscript can be invaluable. My experience with several revisions taught me to self-edit effectively. Keep your copies of "*The Chicago Manual of Style*" and "*The Elements of Style*" handy. An outside editor is beneficial in any circumstance if affordable.

### Publishing

Despite sales success for several years, a few reviews highlighting editorial oversights made me more discerning about editing. While the content's strength may have masked initial errors, the criticisms still sting when considering those early versions.

The journey taught me to prioritize proofreading and editing regardless of constraints. Self-publishing requires wearing multiple hats, the final one being distribution and marketing.

## Distributing

I launched the book in print and digital formats on platforms like Amazon and Apple Books. Later, Ingram Spark became another channel. It's crucial to understand that while Amazon and Apple Books are indeed platforms for sales, they essentially function as international competitors to other retailers such as Barnes & Noble and independent bookstores. Ingram, on the other hand, distributes books globally. Collaborating with them can broaden your reach. While they can facilitate listings on different online platforms, direct dealings can sometimes be more advantageous.

Pricing is another challenge. While ensuring a fair royalty for myself, I aimed for competitive pricing by benchmarking against similar books.

## Marketing and Advertising

A coherent marketing strategy is vital. Advertising, particularly on Amazon, can boost sales. With varying plans available, monitoring expenditure against royalties is essential to ensure profitability.

## Reviews

Reviews significantly influence potential readers. Distributing copies to potential reviewers, especially industry experts, can be an intelligent strategy. While some reviewers charge, their reach and credibility vary. Positive reviews on platforms like Amazon and Publishers Weekly add immense value.

Local media exposure can escalate to national attention. Crafting compelling news releases requires a unique angle to engage media outlets, answering the question, "Why is your publication noteworthy?"

## Sales

"Documentary Directing and Storytelling" has carved its niche in the nonfiction domain. As  one of Real Deal Press's top royalty-earning book, it's been rewarding, though it hasn't brought substantial wealth.

Authors write and publish for myriad reasons. Royalties offer tangible financial benefits. Assuming an average $5.00 royalty for hardback and paperback versions, selling 1,000 copies would yield $5,000, while 10,000 copies would bring in $50,000. Digital versions can also generate similar returns. Selling a book can be a relatively streamlined process for seasoned authors with established names. Their reputation in their field means they likely already possess a loyal audience eagerly awaiting their next release. This existing readership, combined with their credibility, can significantly expedite sales.

In contrast, debut authors face a unique challenge. Without a known name or established track record, simply publishing a great book is seldom enough. To effectively introduce their work to potential readers and sell a thousand copies quickly, they need an aggressive, strategic marketing plan:

**Identify Target Audience**: Understand who would benefit most from your book. Tailor your marketing strategies to appeal directly to this group.

**Leverage social media:** Engage with Twitter, Facebook, and Instagram readers. Regular posts, interactive polls, and sneak peeks can generate buzz.

**Blog Tours:** Collaborate with bloggers in your book's genre. They can review your book, interview you, or host giveaways, offering exposure to their audience.

**Email Marketing**: Build a mailing list and send newsletters with updates, excerpts, and special offers.

**Book Launch Event:** Organize a virtual or physical book launch. It's a great way to introduce your book and engage with readers directly.

**Join Writing Groups:** Engage with other writers and readers in online communities and local writing groups. They can offer support, advice, and potential promotional opportunities.

**Leverage Reviews**: Encourage readers to leave reviews on Amazon and Goodreads. Positive feedback can significantly boost sales.

**Offer Promotions:** Limited-time discounts or bundles can incentivize purchases.

**Engage in Public Speaking:** Offer to speak at seminars, workshops, or podcasts in your field. This positions you as an expert and brings attention to your book.

**Collaborate with Influencers**: If budget allows, collaborate with social media influencers or famous figures in your genre to review or promote your book.

While selling a thousand copies quickly is impressive, focusing on the long game is also essential. Sustainable sales over time often require a mix of aggressive initial marketing and continued, consistent promotional efforts.

Attaining "best-seller" status is nuanced. Lists like The New York Times Best Seller consider more than just sales numbers. For instance, a nonfiction title might need 5,000 to 10,000 first-week sales to feature on this list, with variations based on the season and competitors. Earning $25,000 (at the $5.00 net profit estimate) would mean selling 5,000 copies.

However, other lists, including those of Wall Street Journal, USA Today, and Publishers Weekly, have their criteria. Amazon's dynamic best-seller lists also operate differently.

Achieving a "best-seller" title is noteworthy, but sustained sales and readership longevity often matter more than fleeting list placements.

# BIBLIOGRAPHY


Angelou, Maya. I Know Why the Caged Bird Sings. New York: Ballentine Books. 1969.

Atwan, Robert. The Ten Best American Essays Since 1950. Best American Essay Series. Mariner Books, 2012

Aurelius, Marcus. Meditations, 167 AD. Translated by Richard Graves, 1811.

Baldwin, James. Notes of a Native Son. Harper's Magazine, 1955.

Beard, Jo Ann. The Fourth State of Matter. The New Yorker, 1996.

Capote, Truman. In Cold Blood. New York. Vintage, 1959.

Capote, Truman. In Cold Blood: A True Account of a Multiple Murder and its Consequences. New York Vintage, 1994.

Carreyrou, John. Bad Blood: Secrets and Lies in a Silicon Valley Startup. Knopf, 2018

Carnegie, Dale. How to Win Friends and Influence People. Arrow (Random), 1936

Chernow, Ron. Alexander Hamilton. Penguin Books, 2004

Clear, James. Atomic Habits: An Easy & Proven Way to Build Good Habits & Break Bad Ones. Avery, 2018.

Covey, R. Stephen. The 7 Habits of Highly Effective People. New York. Simon & Schuster, 2018.

Dillard, Annie. Total Eclipse. Antaeus. Harper Perennial, 1982.

Dodes, Lance and Zachary Dodes. The Sober Truth: Debunking the Bad Science Behind 12-Step Programs and the Rehab Industry. Beacon Press, 2014.

Finkel, Michael. The Art Thief, A True Story of Love, Crime, and a Dangerous Obsession. Self-Published, 2023.

Frank, Anne. The Diary of a Young Girl. Pocket Books, 1947, 1952.

Frankl, Victor E. Man's Search for Meaning. Beacon Press, 2006.

Frankopan, Peter. The Silk Roads-A New History of the World. Vintage, 2015.

Gilbert, Elizabeth. Eat, Pray, Love: One Woman's Search for Everything Across Italy, India and Indonesia. River Head Books, 2006.

Graeber, David, and David Wengrow. The Dawn of Everything – A New History of Humanity. New York: Farrar, Straus, and Giroux, 2022.

Grann, David. Killers of the Flower Moon, The Osage Murders, and the Birth of the FBI. Vintage, 2018

Griffiths, David, and Darrel F. Schroeder. Introduction to Quantum Mechanics 3rd Edition. Cambridge University Press, 2019.

Goodell, Jeff. The Water Will Come. Back Bay Books, 2011.

Harari, Yuval Noah. Sapiens: A Brief History of Humankind. New York. Harper Collins, 2015.

Hawking, Stephen. A Brief History of Time. Bantam Books, 1998.

Hill, Napoleon. Think and Grow Rich. TarcherPerigee, 1937.

Hillenbrand, Laura. Unbroken. Ember, 2010.

Housel, Morgan. The Psychology of Money: Timeless Lessons on Wealth, Greed, and Happiness. Harriman House, 2020.

Isaacson, Walter. Steve Jobs. New York. Simon & Schuster, 2011.

Kahneman, Daniel. Thinking, Fast and Slow. Farrar, Straus and Giroux, 2013.

Knight, Phil. Shoe Dog: A Memoir by the Creator of Nike. New York: Scribner, 2016.

Krakauer, Jon. Into the Wild. Anchor Books, 1997.

Kurtz, Keven. The Fascinating Science Book for Kids. Rockridge Press, 2020.

Larson, Erik. The Devil in the White City. New York: Knopf Doubleday Publishing Group, 2003.

Larson, Erik. In the Garden of Beasts. Crown Publishing Group, 2011.

Levitt, Steven D. and Stephen J. Dubner. Freakonomics: A Rogue Economist Explores the Hidden Side of Everything. William Morrow Paperbacks, 2005.

Maddow, Rachel. Blowout: Corrupted Democracy, rogue State Russia, and the Richest, Most Destructive Industry on Earth. Crown, 2019.

Mann, Charles C. 1491: New Revelations of the Americas Before Columbus. Vintage, 2005.

Martin, James R. Actuality Interviewing and Listening. Real Deal Press, 2017, 2023

Martin, James R. Documentary Directing and Storytelling. Real Deal Press, 2018, 2023

McNamara, Michelle. I'll Be Gone in the Dark. Harper Perennial, 2019.

McPhee, John. The Search for Marvin Gardens. The New Yorker,1972.

Rebecca Skloot. The Immortal Life of Henrietta Lacks. Crown, 2011.

Reng, Ronald. A Life Too Short: The Tragedy of Robert Enke. Yellow Jersey, 2011.

Richards, Keith. Life. New York Little Brown, 2010.

Ries, Eric. The Lean Startup. Currency, 2011

Ruiz, Don Miquel. The Four Agreements: A Practical Guide to Personal Freedom. Amber-Allen Publishing Inc, 1977.

Smith, Patti. Just Kids. Ecco, 2010.

Tizon, Alex. My Family's Slave. Essay/Short Story. The Atlantic, 2017.

Wallace, David Foster. Consider the Lobster. Gourmet Magazine, 2004.

Walls, Jeanette. The Glass Castle, Scribner, 2006.

Westover, Tara. Educated: A Memoir. New York. Random House, 2018.

Wilkerson, Isabel. The Warmth of Other Suns. Vintage, 2010.

Winn, Christopher. I Never Knew That About Ireland. Thomas Dunne Books, 2007.

Yongxin, Shi. The Shaolin Temple Story. Real Deal Press, 2023.

*Films*

Shapiro, Dana and Henry-Alex Rubin. MurderBall. Documentary Film. MTV Films; Paramount, 2005.

Martin, James (Jim) R. Wrapped in Steel. PBS Documentary Film. J R Martin Media Inc. 1984 (https://www.youtube.com/watch?v=vq_c-XXU1Tk)

# Index

## Q

# R

## U

## V

207